UNLOCKING
THE SECRETS OF YOUR
CHILDHOOD MEMORIES

WORKBOOK

UNLOCKING
THE SECRETS OF YOUR
CHILDHOOD MEMORIES

WORKBOOK

DR. KEVIN LEMAN
& RANDY CARLSON

A JANET THOMA BOOK

Thomas Nelson Publishers
Nashville

Part Two:
You Can Change the Story

All the World's a Stage

". . . , And all the men and women merely players."

Shakespeare was right. Everyone's life is a play.

At birth, the curtain rises. After a moment of awkward infancy, the bright spotlight of your own perception begins to illuminate the stage. In that instant of recognition, a special camera starts to roll. Its selective lens perpetually records every movement, every character on the platform—from *your* personal point of view.

Yet unlike Shakespeare's plays, your life is not a well-crafted script. It is, rather, a series of well-intentioned but often mishandled improvisations. In short, we make it up as we go along. However, that doesn't mean that your life is without structure. The circumstances of each scene you play are based on the combined experiences of every prior scene you've played. Therefore, life is really not "acting" but "re-acting" to *your remembered* reactions of others.

Your memory sets the stage. It controls your mood. It dictates the words you say and the reactions you display. If you can understand the motives—the behind-the-scenes reasons why you remember certain things a particular way—if you can learn how to put those memories in their proper context, then you can actually change your story.

It can be done. However, to ensure success you must be willing to follow the stage instructions of the Master Director, God, and be ready to boldly explore the pleasant and the imperfect scenes of your past.

The *earlier* the memory, the closer you'll be to the source of your personal perception. The more you recall of your past, the easier it will be to understand your current situation. If you go back as far as to unlock the secrets of your *childhood memories*, you can adjust the future direction of your life's play. You can improve your performance.

Before the next scene goes too far, take a moment out of your ad-lib existence and schedule an intermission. Take the time . . . to remember.

Part One

Setting the Stage

"The child you once were, you still are."
—Dr. Kevin Leman

"Memories are the fingerprints of your personality."
—Randy Carlson

Chapter One

Rewinding Your Mind

"To be alive is to have a past."

They say that the first rule of acting is to understand the basic nature of your character. In order to make a performance believable, an actor evaluates every scene of a play to discover the underlying emotions of his or her role. The mark of a successful stage player is the ability to comprehend the subtle, behind-the-scenes reasons their characters do what they do.

If, for instance, the script calls for Sheriff Tex automatically to reach for his gun when he hears the jingle of a pair of spurs, a good actor will likewise instinctively react to the noise. The prepared performer knows that in the character's mind lurks the painful memory of a distant time when that subtle jingle was the only forewarning of a deadly gunslinger's entrance.

The first rule of acting is to understand the basic nature of your character.

Those between-the-lines reasons, however, are not always evident in the script. In such cases the actors themselves often resort to creating their own "backstory" (an imagined history) to give their onstage actions clarity, reason, and purpose.

In real life, we do the same thing.

At one time or another, we have all tried to understand the basic nature of *our* character. Each one of us searches between the lines and wonders why we do the things we do. *Who am I? How did I become this person? Why am I afraid of taking risks? Why don't I have friends? Why is it hard for me to communicate?* When these questions are not readily answered, we often resort to creating imaginary backstories (false histories resulting in misplaced blame) to help explain away our broken relationships and mishandled lives.

Like actors, we are each players on the world's stage, yet there is no need for us to create desperate backstories to clarify why we do the things we do; for from the moment of birth, every scene we have ever played has been stored away for future reference. The very answers you seek today about yourself and your present life have been meticulously recorded and cataloged . . . in your memories.

The very answers you seek today about yourself and your present life have been meticulously recorded and cataloged . . . in your memories.

Those unique remembrances, along with the words and feelings you use to describe them, are the tools by which you, through this workbook, can actually discover who you truly are and why. If you want to know the nature of your present-day character, you must evaluate the past scenes of your life. If you are looking for what you must do to change your future, you must explore the subtle, between-the-lines reasons that brought you to this point. "The wisdom of the prudent," Proverbs 14:8 states, "is to understand his way." To discover where you are going, you must first know where you've been. To be alive is to have a past.

In *Unlocking the Secrets of Your Childhood Memories*, we make the reader a promise, *"Tell us about your earliest childhood memories, and we'll tell you about yourself today."* We make that same promise to you in this workbook. We are confident that if you stick with us, you will have a better understanding of where you are going and how to get there. We are certain that you will uncover the basic nature of your character and comprehend the proper direction to take your life's story, because you will know—for a fact—how it all began.

As we go, we'll give you a chance to answer some specific questions. We've also left room in the margins for you to jot notes, journal, or record memories as they arise in your mind.

Let's start the process of unlocking your past by "rewinding" your memory.

Circle the number rating that you feel best defines the general nature of your childhood.

I enjoyed my childhood.

0	1	2	3	4	5	6	7	8	9	10
Never		Very Seldom		Sometimes		Almost Always				Constantly

As a child, I felt a sense of belonging.

0	1	2	3	4	5	6	7	8	9	10
Never		Very Seldom		Sometimes		Almost Always				Constantly

My childhood was a "magical time."

0	1	2	3	4	5	6	7	8	9	10
Never		Very Seldom		Sometimes		Almost Always				Constantly

Did you ever feel like running away from home?

0	1	2	3	4	5	6	7	8	9	10
Never	Very Seldom		Sometimes			Almost Always				Constantly

Did you want to grow up?

0	1	2	3	4	5	6	7	8	9	10
Never	Very Seldom		Sometimes			Almost Always				Constantly

Do you ever wish that you could relive your childhood?

0	1	2	3	4	5	6	7	8	9	10
Never	Very Seldom		Sometimes			Almost Always				Constantly

How you answered these six questions discloses a great deal about how you view your early life.

What insights about yourself do these initial answers reveal to you?

To assist in the rewinding process, let's begin to fine-tune your focus. Answer the following questions with as much detail as possible.

As a child, what was your "Best Day"?

What was the "Worst Day" of your childhood?

Helpful Hints for Rewinding

The Earlier the Memory the Better

Most psychologists agree that children make many important decisions in their first five or six years. Within those first few years most youngsters create their own answers to those classic questions Who am I? What must I do? What is good? What is bad? Children create their own logic, which makes each of them different from any other human being.

Hence, each of us has our own private logic. Through trial and error we test everything to see if it fits with our emotional need to belong in life. If it does, we make a mental note to keep that feeling or behavior for later use. If what we do or feel ceases to fit our need to belong, we throw it out. In the process of all this choosing and discarding, small pieces of our personality fall into place.

These small but revealing pieces of our makeup are more clearly visible in our earliest childhood memories because they are not cluttered with the defense mechanisms we have learned as adults. Recent memories are more likely to reflect the person you would like to be or think you are, instead of the *real* person who was molded long ago in your childhood. Early memories can't be fooled. They picture the real you, how you actually perceive life and live it, whether you realize it or not.

Early memories can't be fooled. They picture the real you.

What is the earliest image or event you can remember? It doesn't have to be an entire scene. It could be just a flash, a moment in time, a piece of a puzzle.

The More *Early Memories the Better*

You can learn a lot from a single memory, but in most cases you can learn even more from several. Early childhood memories are like threads woven together to form the fabric of understanding. The more early memories, the more threads; the more threads, the stronger the fabric; the stronger the fabric, the more *personal* the insight and the clearer the picture.

What is the second earliest image or event you can remember?

The Memories Must Be Yours Alone

A parent or a family friend may have told you, *"I'll never forget the time when you . . ."* so many times that you are no longer certain whether you remember the scene or just recall having it told to you.

If you can remember feeling a specific emotion and can see an actual picture of the scene in your mind, the memory most likely is yours. Use this simple test to separate real memories from vivid, secondhand stories: Close your eyes and ask yourself two questions: What did I feel? (Was I happy, peaceful, afraid, loved, lonely, hurt?) and What do I see? (Do I see Mom, Dad, my crib, my house, my yard?)

Complete the following phrase.

In my first memory, I saw (. . . *Daddy standing above me, holding a big red balloon.*)

In my first memory, *I felt (. . . loved when Daddy stooped down and handed me the balloon.)*

In my second memory, I saw

In my second memory, I felt

Each Memory Must Describe
Specific Events

It is easier to recall generalities rather than specifics. A general memory might begin, *"After school, we would always . . ."* or *"Just about every Saturday Dad and I would . . ."* To get a real memory, you must focus on a specific event or a specific day. For example: *"I remember one day I was riding in the front seat of Grampa's car, when a big truck drove by and honked its horn—loud."* Or, *"I'll never forget the day when my third-grade teacher asked me to clean the blackboard."*

A good example of a vivid memory belongs to Bart. His recollection is not only an early one, it is his alone, and it is specific:

It was the morning of my fourth birthday. My mother dressed me in warm knee pants, dark socks that came halfway up my little legs, and a pair of white hard-soled shoes. Escorting me to the front door of our house, she pointed down the street to a building on the corner and told me that everyone was waiting there for my party. Scooting me out the door, she said, "You're late. Watch out for cars. Be careful." It was the first time I ever recall going anywhere by myself. I remember walking on the gravel along the side of the road and feeling the little stones crunch underneath my shoes.

But when I think of this memory, the first thing that comes to mind is walking along that roadside, holding up three little fingers in front of my face, and repeating over and over, "I once was three . . ." then I raised another finger, "and now I'm four . . . I once was three, and now I'm four . . ."

Are the mental cobwebs clearing? Let's see. Read the following questions slowly and let your mind wander a bit. Chances are you'll come across a thought or two that will get your mind's wheels turning.

Describe an early birthday party or a memorable holiday.

Describe one or two of your elementary school teachers (especially first or second grade).

Why do they stand out?

Do you remember the day you learned to ride a bike? What happened?

Another excellent example of a childhood memory comes from Kevin Leman's earliest recollection:

> I was about three. . . . I was banging on the front door of my house. I wanted to get in and go potty, but the door was locked. I know it was a Sunday morning because the big thick Sunday paper sat on the front steps. I don't recall why I'd gone outside, but when I wanted to get back in, I found the door locked. So I stood there pounding and calling for someone to let me in. But no one heard me before I messed in my pants.

Notice the specific detail and the implication of urgency in Kevin's memory. It is important to not only see the event replayed in your mind, but it is helpful to also reexperience the emotions of the event as well.

Now that we have primed your "memory pump," focus your thoughts on some of your earliest recollections and write them down in the spaces provided.

Note: Your earliest memories are full of the emotions you had as a child. Don't concern yourself with editing them. Simply write down what you remember and how you felt. Your perception of the scene is as important as the event itself. Try to recall not only what happened but how you reacted. This exercise is to help *improve you,* not blame others. Try to concentrate on the years prior to age eight. The memories you choose don't have to be exciting or unusual—they just have to be *yours*.

Childhood Memory #1   My approximate age: ___
I remember

The clearest part of my recollection is

As I think about this memory I feel

Childhood Memory #2   **My approximate age:** ___
I remember

The clearest part of my recollection is

As I think about this memory I feel

Stuck? That's okay. Approximately 20 percent of the population has trouble remembering events that took place prior to age ten. The fact that you are having difficulty with early events says something about you, your past, and your present. However, let's not get ahead of ourselves.

For now, try taking a slow, imaginary walk through your childhood home. Make sure you visit each room. What do you see?

- What about Christmastime? Can you recall a special Christmas or Hanukkah?
- A special present you received?
- Remember any special family or school out-ings?

- What were your brothers and sisters like? Did you get along? Why or why not?
- What did you do at bedtime when you were little?
- What frightened you as a child? Can you remember some of your "scariest" experiences?
- What were some of your most embarrassing moments? Who and what were involved?

Childhood Memory #3   **My approximate age:** ____

I remember

The clearest part of my recollection is

As I think about this memory I feel

Drawing blanks in the blanks? Let's try another approach. Complete the following sentences.

As a child I was happiest when . . .

As a child I felt safest when . . .

As a child I felt loved whenever . . .

As a child I was loneliest when . . .

Write down any insights you have noticed.

As you begin your exploration of memory lane, keep in mind two more hints.

Focus on the Clearest Part of Your Memory

Consider the memory of a hypothetical seven-year-old boy. In his imaginary recollection, the boy remembers an after-school bike ride that ended abruptly when his front wheel hit a curb. He recalls the sudden crash, the pain of a skinned elbow, and crying. He remembers his mother, who obviously heard his sobs, running out of the house, gathering him in her arms, and kissing the skinned spot. He also remembers her helping him back up on his bike so that he could try again.

The main point of this contrived memory illustrates many of the necessary requirements of memory exploration:

- It is an early scene, age seven.
- The memory belongs to the boy. There is no mention of, "My mother once told me about the time . . ."
- The recollection zeros in on a specific event—there is no generalization like, "I used to ride my bike a lot after school . . ."

You need to zero in on your memories. If the bike incident had happened to you and had been filmed; which moment in the action—which frame of the film—would be most vivid to you? Would it be the fall itself? Would it be the moment your mother arrived to offer you comfort? Or maybe it would be the instant she gave you a little helpful push to get started again.

With this exercise in mind, write down the clearest part of your *first* memory.

Attach Feeling to the Clearest Part of the Memory

Continuing with the illustration of the bike wreck, if the clearest part of the memory is falling down, you might attach to it a feeling of fear, hurt, anger, or embarrassment. Yet if the clearest moment is the encouragement your mother gave you, then the primary feeling might be determination, "I'll never quit!"

Assigning a feeling to your memories is the last crucial step in the exploration process. If you are having trouble with identifying your childhood emotions, it could mean you have difficulty getting in touch with your feelings as an adult.

Try attaching a *specific feeling* to your first memory. Close your eyes and refocus on the clearest part of the scene. How did you feel at that moment?

Your physical behavior is crucial as well. Look for a *recurring physical posture* in your memories. Were you usually standing, sitting, running?

You can also get some insight into your feelings by your *attitudes toward adults*. How do you recall feeling about authority?

Like an actor on stage, most people feel that they must be in control of themselves and their surroundings in order to give the best possible performance. A lack of security in childhood often intensifies that desire for control in adulthood.

Is it important for you to be in control?

In childhood, did you ever feel threatened by change?

As a child, when you sensed that things were not going "your way," how did you react? Check the statements that best describe your response:

_____ I felt that I would never measure up.

_____ I thought, "If I would only do _____, then everything would be fine."

_____ I was guilt ridden and often wanted to punish myself.

_____ When confronted, I often denied involvement, or blamed others.

_____ I liked to be led. If someone else told me to do it, then it wasn't my fault.

_____ I felt that others were responsible to meet my needs and assist me in reaching my goals.

_____ I tended to avoid or escape responsibility for my actions.

_____ I shrugged off consequences of my behavior and went on as if nothing were wrong.

_____ I excused my conduct by feigning sickness.

_____ I looked for ways to improve.

Being vulnerable and trusting others requires an ability to give up control. In the scenes of daily life, there are crisis times when that need to be in charge conflicts with a sudden, sometimes panic-like demand for extra guidance.

Today, when you lose control of a situation or person, how do you feel?

Think of the last time you were *not* in control, how did you respond?

In those times of "panic," an actor relinquishes control of the stage and confers with the director. In life, during those times of sudden uncertainty, we, the players on this world stage also have a guide to turn to, God, the Master Director. He is the only One who can see the "big picture" of your storyline. He has the knowledge and power to "fix" the scene in which you are currently playing. Giving up your control to His guidance is the surest way to unlock the secrets of your childhood and your future.

The Bible, God's Master Script, encourages, *"Cast all of your anxiety on [God] because he cares for you."* And Psalm 46:1 informs us that *"God is our refuge and strength,/A very present help in trouble."* In the scenes of your daily life, does God *feel* like a refuge?

_____ Yes _____ Sometimes _____ No

Let's take a closer look now at the memories you've written so far. Let the spotlight of your personal perception shine on the stage. Do any of the scenes you have recalled share consistent themes or emotions? If so, list them here.

In life, during those times of sudden uncertainty, we have a guide to turn to—God.

Do these consistencies have any effect on your actions today?

If you answered yes, you are on your way to unlocking the secrets of your childhood memories. Within your recollections there is at work an underlying, unconscious logic. This perpetual, automatic mode of reasoning has helped shape the basic nature of your character. And in the next section, you will discover how this intuitive *consistency* can be put to use to actually begin changing the direction of your life's story—*today!*

Follow Your Stage Directions

If "all the world is a stage" and we are the actors, then it is important that we not only explore the true nature of our character, we must also pay close attention to the instructions provided for us in the script itself. These helpful stage directions tell you *where, when, and what* our character should do on the platform. In the context of a few well-chosen words, you're told what to wear, whether to stand or sit, when to move and even how to react in the process. These convenient guides suggest whether you should laugh, cry, fly into a rage, or gently caress. In effect, these snips of words and phrases are the subtle signposts that help us to navigate our way through a scene and enhance our performance.

In the course of daily life, however, such helpful hints are not so readily evident. Most of the time we end up ad-libbing our way through difficult moments. Ironically, we never seem to realize our need for direction until we are thrust into the middle of an awkward situation. It is in those moments of panic that we usually recognize our deficiency. And in the context of that anxiety we tend to grapple for an answer with one hand, while struggling for self-control with the other. In short, we make life up as we go along, and most of the time we have no idea what way that should be.

Nevertheless in life, just as in a artistic script, if you know where to look for them, you'll find the signposts for direction everywhere. Art is in itself a reflection of life's do's and don'ts. Down through the ages, dramatic plays, books, and historical accounts have illustrated the lessons of life. Shakespeare, for one, was a master at holding up a mirror to humanity. Even today his scripts blatantly illustrate the full spectrum human achievement and destruction. There is indeed much we can learn about ourselves from his emotion-filled plots and characters. However, the best illustration of life's do's and don'ts were recognized by a simple fisherman who walked the earth's stage close to two millennia ago.

His observant words and phrases have stood the test of time and helped to improve the performances of countless characters. In fact, his own life is an example of how an insignificant player can change his story and earn an honorable mention on history's marquis. The man's name was Simon Peter.

As he approached the closing chapter of his own story, Peter reflected on the eventful scenes of his time in the spotlight. Reminiscing on his life, just as we are beginning to do with our childhood memories, he evaluated the lessons he had learned along the way. The sum of those experiences he committed to paper. And it is those few well-chosen words, those simple "Stage Directions" you are going to examine throughout the course of your memory exploration.

In the context of your quest to improve your onstage character, Peter's suggestions are indeed helpful hints to follow: "Giving all diligence, add to your faith virtue; and to virtue knowledge; and to knowledge temperance; and to temperance patience; and to patience godliness; and to godliness brotherly kindness; and to brotherly kindness charity. . . . Wherefore the rather, brethren, give diligence to make your calling and election sure: for if you do these things, you shall never fall" (2 Peter 1:5–7, 10).

These "directions" tell you *what* your character *should* do on the platform of your life. They contain the signposts capable of guiding you through your memories and the lessons they hold—the attributes that will assist you through those awkward moments when it seems as though you have forgotten your lines and are not sure which way to turn.

In these instructions, Peter cautions future performers that if they refuse to consider these "additions" to their character, they are "blind, and cannot see afar off" (v. 9 KJV). For you to truly want to change the course of your life, you must be willing to see the path you have traveled, accept that you have strayed off course, if you have, and be obliged to make alterations. If you refuse to examine your life—the scenes you have played—there is no way you can see "afar off." It is impossible to alter your future development successfully if you are "blind" to your faulty past.

The fact that you have opened this workbook and are voluntarily reading *this* page proves that you, like Peter, are willing to look back on your life and learn. Therefore, if all the world is a stage and you are a player, it is important that you strive to daily improve your character. The surest way to achieve that goal is to pay attention to the do's and don'ts that will enhance your performance. And as any good actor will tell you, *that* is following the stage directions.

With that sense of purpose in mind, let's look at the first of Simon's suggested character "additions." It is an attribute which, by the way, you have *already begun* to display.

Stage Direction #1: Diligence

Diligence is not just an action but an attitude. The task of improving yourself and your relationships with others must begin with the right mental motivation. Your frame of mind must portray a willingness to work untiringly, zealously to fulfill your intended purpose. Diligence provides you with that desire.

Here at the beginning, you must realize this voyage you've initiated into your memories concerns more than just an ambition to learn about yourself. This inward journey is also about your need to empower others with an understanding of who you are. Such a long-suffering endeavor can only be accomplished with a steady dose of diligence.

This trait of persistency supplies you with the mental motivation necessary to build a relationship from scratch. It is the sustaining mortar that bolsters you in the often tedious process of rebuilding broken lives and crumbling friendships.

The great thinker Henry David Thoreau once commented, "If one advances confidently in the direction of his dreams, and endeavors to live the life which he has imagined, he will meet with a success unexpected in common hours." Diligence is the ability to "advance confidently." It is the positive ingredient of every determined soul, for it constantly whispers the unwavering directive, "No matter how long it takes, *keep on, keepin' on!*"

This positive sense of perseverance was once displayed on a talk show examining the topic of "aging gracefully." As the studio lights went on, a smiling host took his microphone out into the TV audience and approached an old man sitting on the aisle. Thrusting the microphone into the gentleman's face, the host assumed a well-practiced look of sincerity and asked, "How about you, sir? What do you attribute your long life to?"

Pondering the question, the old fellow wrapped his wrinkled hand around his cane and pulled his weathered body to its feet. A broad grin crossed his furrowed face and his bespectacled eyes lit up with the memories of a lengthy life. "Well, in all my 88 years," he said, turning confidently toward the camera, "I can truthfully say that I've *never* been down."

Diligence . . . constantly whispers . . . "no matter how long it takes, keep on keepin' on."

A young man sitting across the aisle wrinkled his brow upon hearing those words. To him, the old man's declaration was disturbing. It wasn't what he expected to hear at all.

After the show, as the small group began to file out of the studio, the young fellow caught up with the slow-moving gentleman and asked, "How can you claim what you said, back there? I don't understand. I've been doin' all I know to do to keep my family fed and the rent paid. And still, despite my best efforts, I feel as if the world is sitting on my shoulders. Most of the time I feel like giving up! How can you say that you've never been down? I've been down seven times, *this* week!"

Looking up at the young man's puzzled frown, the venerable gentleman grinned just a little. "Son, it's all a matter of perspective," he explained, patting his wrinkled hand against the young man's flustered face. "You see, I'm always up—or gettin' up."

The positive attitude exhibited by that old man is a quality consistent with persistence. A person demonstrating the characteristics of diligence strives to avoid any notion of negativity. They value their aspiration much more than their perspiration. No doubt it was an individual of such endurance who coined the phrase, *"No pain, no gain."*

Diligence is a ninety-pound dreamer staring into a mirror, tirelessly pumping iron, fully expecting one day to see Arnold Schwarzeneggar staring back. Diligence is a long-distance runner who, though weary, continually puts one foot in front of the other to reach the finish line first. Diligence is an attitude of action, instilling one's character with the daring incentive to try and the courageous strength to stick with it.

If it wasn't for the attribute of diligence the world would be a much different place. Had Christopher Columbus not demonstrated the positive perspective to see that the world was round, and the untiring persistence to "keep on keepin' on" until someone gave him the boats to prove it, chances are we would not be living as we do. Or for that matter, we might not exist at all.

In the context of your own journey of discovery, it is vital that you follow your stage directions and acquire the characteristic of diligence. You don't have to worry if you can't remember everything in your childhood. Instead, concentrate on the events you can recall. Diligently search through your memories and learn from them how your character has developed. You are going to be dealing with aspects of your personality you have never before confronted. Nevertheless, you must endeavor to discover even those things about yourself that are not pleasant, because, like Columbus, only through such persistent, courageous searching will *your* new world appear.

Remember, diligence is not just sticking with a project until it is finished but maintaining a positive attitude throughout the tedious process. Despite the hurdles you may encounter along your memory journey, diligence can help you to sustain the upbeat outlook necessary to "keep on keepin' on."

Shakespeare once observed that, "There is nothing good or bad, but thinking makes it so." Therefore, if you want a constructive change in your life, you must first decide to try. Your conscious choice to improve by perusing the secrets in your childhood memories is indeed a "good" step in the right direction. However, your thinking must also include the resolve to stick with it. And that requires the added attitude of endurance, long-suffering, and persistence. Such positive thinking requires diligence.

It is good to keep in mind Peter's suggestion of this particular attribute, for diligence is the ingredient of every determined soul. Despite what tomorrow may bring, it is perseverance that constantly whispers, "I'm always up—or getting up."

Chapter Two

Subconscious Consistencies

"Self-exploration does not change you, it unmasks you."

No one just happens to pick a particular memory from among the millions of experiences of childhood and adolescence and forget all the others.

One of the significant truths about memory exploration is that we all decide on a subconscious level what we will remember and what we will block out. Although every experience of our lives has been filed away in our brains, we tend to make use only of the ones that best express our personal view. There is no official term for this sorting process, but we like to call it the *Law of Creative Consistency:*

People tend to remember only those events from early childhood that are consistent with their present view of themselves and the world around them.

We all decide on a subconscious level what we will re-member.

Are there any consistently recurring locations in your memories, such as school, home, a special hiding place?

Are there any recurring people in your memories, such as parents, brothers, sisters, grandparents, neighbors, classmates?

In your memories, are you usually an *observer* (watching the action from the sidelines) or a *participant* (in the middle of the activity, personally involved)?

Place your initials next to the consistent themes that run through your memories.

_____ Fear/Worry

_____ Low Self-Esteem

_____ Aggressiveness

_____ Shyness

_____ Submissiveness

_____ Humiliation

_____ Selfishness

_____ Rebellion

_____ Resourcefulness

_____ Acute Self-Consciousness

How do these themes influence your present behavior?

Randy Carlson's early memories graphically illustrate the presence of consistent themes:

I must have been about six or seven when my parents bought me a little red bike—a *girl's* bike. My dad had to have a bar welded on it because I wouldn't be seen on a girl's bike.

He also recalls:

I had two big brothers, one six years and one ten years my senior. They treated me like the "little dumb kid." One day they were both in my oldest brother's bedroom playing with their shortwave radio. I walked in but wasn't too welcome. My oldest brother warned, "You better get out of here, Fat Butt" (their favorite pet name for me because I was heavy for my age). Then he added, "You've got three seconds to get out of here, or I'm gonna shoot you with my BB gun." My brother grabbed his air rifle from behind the door, and as I ran out of the room, he cocked the gun and shot me in my ample behind. I felt angry, ostracized, and humiliated.

Do you see the consistencies in Randy's childhood memories? His early life reveals an obvious recurrence of fear, humiliation, and a strong concern about the opinions of others.

Randy readily acknowledges that the consistent themes of his early memories continue to crop up in his life today. "I'm a careful, cautious person," Randy admits, "who longs so badly for security that I sometimes have to force myself to take bold steps and risk humiliation. I often nearly drive my wife crazy with my concern about others' opinions of me and my work."

What do the consistent traits you initialed above tell you about yourself?

Whoops! From your description, it looks like your character could use a little polishing—but then again, so could everyone's. All the world's a stage, and each of us, at one time or another, has reacted badly to the slings and arrows of life's misfortunes. Yet, despite the fact that those themes are repeated over and over throughout our lives, we seem to ignore their cues and continually blow our lines.

Self-exploration does not change you, it unmasks you. It is up to you to do the changing.

The themes that reoccur in our lives should tip us off to the flaws in our performance, but sometimes they don't. Simply put, we are often blinded by our prevailing view of ourselves so we don't see our personality flaws until it is too late.

Pretend you are a drama critic assigned to review *you*. Compose a colorful critique, describing your present-day character in the ongoing play of life.

In the role of _____, I see a character
(your name)
who can only be described as

The only way to improve the performance of this character is

There is a fact of life that every actor knows: No matter how hard you try, you can't escape your reviews: Whether you get a standing ovation or you are laughed off the stage, you have to live with the results of your performance. You cannot change the past.

No matter how hard you try, you can't escape your reviews.

Yet, despite the unavoidable pain of those negative memories, *you can learn* from your past experiences. In fact, the very process of facing your bad reviews head-on can improve the quality of your next performance. But that act of face-to-face confrontation is a choice *you* have to make.

To improve or not to improve, *that* is the question. You can either sit back and suffer the slings and arrows of your past mistakes, or face them and grow.

It is remarkable what you can accomplish if you set your mind to it. See yourself as an *improving* adult, not some poor thing who's been mistreated and can't get over it. *Self-pity is the enemy of maturity.* Take responsibility for yourself.

Don't expect someone else to set your character straight. That's *your* job. And don't wait for God to wave a magic wand and make everything better. The Master Director is always within reach, just beyond the footlights, ever ready to assist in your refinement. But it is up to *you* to heed His stage directions, learn from your past, and experience the actual process of refinement yourself.

Facing your bad reviews with dignity and a sense of responsibility is the beginning of self-exploration and change.

Childhood memories and the evaluation of those past recollections are God's built-in tools to assist you in unlocking the full potential of your character. If you take this exploration seriously, you can alter your circumstances and even improve your future performance. You have it within you to influence effectively your character's development. If you can boldly face your past, you can change your future!

It's As Easy As Riding a Bike

The exploration you are beginning is like learning to ride a bicycle. The combined terror and elation of that childhood experience is a memory most of us can recall.

Let's go back to that hypothetical seven-year-old bike rider from chapter 1, back to when he mustered the courage to finally take off his training wheels. When a child decides to take that next step in his development and ride his bike "for real," his arms and legs are not the only parts of him that are put to the test; his memory is also tested.

Once the training wheels have been removed, a trusted adult (usually the parent) holds the two-wheeler steady while the child climbs on and grasps the handle bars in a brave, but white-knuckled grip. The parent then begins to push the bike forward, slowly at first. As the child picks up the pace, the parent lovingly whispers words of encouragement and instructions: *"Watch where you are going. It's alright, I've got you. Look straight ahead. Peddle! Faster! Keep peddling!"* Somewhere along the way the parent lets go. But he or she still runs alongside offering the wobbly rider support and guidance.

As with all beginners, the child inevitably falls, skinning a knee. Nevertheless, undaunted, the child mounts the bike again. Over and over the youngster repeats the process until his consistent failures unconsciously register a pattern in his memory. He adjusts his technique to compensate for his mistakes, learning from his memories how to remain upright. Eventually, the child learns what to do and what *not* to do in order to stay balanced. And all the while hovering close by, the proud parent maintains a watchful eye, just in case the child should call.

The act of learning to ride a bike is very much like learning about yourself through childhood memories. Like the consistent mistakes which cause the bike rider to fall, you, too, have character consistencies which have repeatedly thrown your life out of balance. The exercise of recalling scenes from your past causes your pattern of falls and scrapes to register in your conscious mind. The discovery of those consistent traits will help you to learn what to do and what *not* to do to adjust your behavior. And in time, that knowledge will lead you to a more balanced life.

Like the youngster, you may also be a little "white-knuckled" about this journey you are beginning. Here at the start, you may even wobble a little, uncertain of what you might discover. But you don't have to make this journey alone. There is someone you can trust standing close by. With a watchful eye, God, the Master Director, is ready and willing to offer you words of encouragement and instruction. Like a concerned parent (Ps. 103:13), He will follow along beside you. All you need to do is call and He will gladly guide you in your quest to unlock the secrets of your childhood memories.

Character Consistency

You must understand, however, that though your unlocked memories help to adjust your performance, this conscious knowledge *will not change your original nature*. Regardless of how bad your reviews become, no matter how much you want to wipe the slate clean and start fresh with a new identity, *you cannot stop being you.*

The bike rider's consistencies are short-term flaws in his physical posture. Your character consistencies however, are long-term traits, permanently ingrained into your psychological attitude.

Your basic personality is already established. Your uniquely individual, God-given traits originated in the cradle, and by the time you were four or five, your identity was as permanent as the grain in a piece of wood.

The little boy or girl you once were, you still are. You *can't* recast your character.

The famous actor Jimmy Stewart, for example, played many diverse roles during his long career, and he adapted himself well to each character he portrayed. Yet, though his costumes ranged from a lawyer's three-piece suit to the dusty chaps of a cowpuncher, his underlying identity *remained*—James Maitland Stewart. Always lingering underneath the studio makeup was the enduring human nature of a lanky, likable Pennsylvania boy.

To explore your character consistencies, think about how the child in your memories is *still* alive today. Check each of the statements that are true.

In My Memories . . .	**In My Adult Life . . .**
___ I felt alone	___ I feel alone in a crowd
___ I felt fear	___ I constantly worry

In My Memories . . .	In My Adult Life . . .
⎯⎯ I recall detail	⎯⎯ I am detail intensive
⎯⎯ I recall touching, colors, smells	⎯⎯ I am resourceful/ creative
⎯⎯ I felt nothing at all	⎯⎯ I find it difficult to define my emotions
⎯⎯ I was active	⎯⎯ I am always on the go
⎯⎯ I was passive	⎯⎯ I tend to observe rather than participate
⎯⎯ I felt safe	⎯⎯ Financial/ physical security is a top priority
⎯⎯ I felt the need to please others	⎯⎯ I don't like to rock the boat
⎯⎯ I was often angry	⎯⎯ I am often angry

Now take a moment to add to this list. Write down any additional consistencies you have personally noticed in your character.

In My Memories . . .   **In My Adult Life . . .**

⎯⎯⎯⎯⎯⎯⎯⎯⎯⎯   ⎯⎯⎯⎯⎯⎯⎯⎯⎯⎯

⎯⎯⎯⎯⎯⎯⎯⎯⎯⎯   ⎯⎯⎯⎯⎯⎯⎯⎯⎯⎯

⎯⎯⎯⎯⎯⎯⎯⎯⎯⎯   ⎯⎯⎯⎯⎯⎯⎯⎯⎯⎯

⎯⎯⎯⎯⎯⎯⎯⎯⎯⎯   ⎯⎯⎯⎯⎯⎯⎯⎯⎯⎯

Another consistency to consider is that this world is made up of two kinds of people, *givers and takers*. Each of us falls predominantly into one of these two specific categories.

A taker tends to be aggressive, while a giver is less assertive. A taker tends to be more attractive, while givers are less so. A giver seldom breaks off relationships, takers often do. Takers are in control, givers have less control.

Takers have shorter fuses than givers. For example, a taker will endure a conversation or social event only as long as he or she is interested. A giver, on the other hand, will stick around afterward to help clean up. Takers have needs like everyone else, but they place those needs above serving others.

The attitude of a classic taker is cleverly illustrated in the cartoon antics of Fred Flintstone. *Wilma! What's for dinner? I'm starved!* Fred is always wondering, *"What's in it for me?"* He is constantly contriving new, elaborate ways to become rich and famous, to get even with his boss, to beat the system. Yet, to be fair, most of Fred's schemes manage to contain a trickle-down effect that includes his family. Still, when it comes to winning the grand prize at the local bowling tournament, Wilma, Pebbles, Betty, and Barney had best get out of the way—*especially* if the grand prize is food.

Barney Rubble, on the other hand, is definitely a giver. Little Barney is always there, ready, willing, and able to help neighbor Fred execute his latest scheme. Without ever giving it a second thought, Barney would sell his car to bail Fred out of a jam. He never complains. He never has something else to do. Barney is always the one who asks, "What do ya want me to do now, Fred?" Fred is always the one who says, "See ya later, Barn'."

Are you a consistent giver or a taker? Before you answer, complete the following statements.

In childhood, my first consideration was . . .

—— "What can I do for others?"
—— "What's in it for me?"

As an adult, my first consideration is usually . . .

—— "What can I do for others?"
—— "What's in it for me?"

As you can see, the grain is set. You can't recast your character. Your basic human nature is something you must struggle with all of your life. But what if you don't like the way your grain is slanted? Can anything be done about it? **Yes,** but only if you are willing to be totally honest with yourself—about yourself.

When you unlock the secrets hiding in your childhood memories, your discoveries are not always pleasant. But remember, *knowledge is power*. Through your memories, you can identify your negative character traits, learn how to strengthen your consistent weaknesses, and avoid your usual traps. In doing so, you can actually affect the life scenes your character plays.

Right now, your personal identity may seem as ho-hum as Jimmy Stewart's uneventful, midwestern childhood. Even so, just like Jimmy, you, too, have the ability to adapt your unique nature to as many varied scenes as life can throw at you. You can learn to adjust your behavior and change the plot of your life's story.

With that in mind, truthfully list the *negative* character traits you feel need adapting.

To begin the adapting process, you must first learn to accept yourself as you are. It is important to admit to yourself, *without condemnation,* the negative elements that make up your adult personality.

Condemnation is self-inflicted sentencing. It is like being blindfolded and placed in a room where the furniture has been haphazardly arranged. Without the benefit of lights or any prior knowledge of the room's design, you are told to place the furniture back in its proper location. Such a task is virtually impossible. Both the room and you are destined to remain in a mutual state of disrepair.

The identification of your negative character traits should not lead to condemnation but rather to the cleansing process of *conviction.* This procedure of self-exonerating admission is simply agreeing with and professing the truth that you are not perfect and you need to change.

You can learn to adjust your behavior and change the plot of your life's story.

Conviction is putting the same man in the same disheveled room, only this time the blindfold has been removed and the light of truth has been switched on. As before, he is told to straighten up the mess, but on this go 'round, he is given the Master Director's Blueprint to help him do the job right. God's Master script, the Bible, assures us that "If we confess our sins, He is faithful and just to forgive us our sins and to cleanse us from all unrighteousness" (1 John 1:9).

Now that you understand the importance of truthfully facing who you are, quickly read through the following list of positive traits and check those that are important to you. Then go back and put your initial next to those attributes you feel you currently possess.

____ *Teamwork:* working well with others

____ *Independence:* doing things on your own when necessary

____ *Obedience:* respecting and submitting to authority

____ *Initiative:* seeing what needs to be done and doing it

____ *Supportiveness:* encouraging others to do their best

____ *Perseverance:* completing what you start

____ *Motivation:* wanting something, then doing it

____ *Kindness:* showing caring concern for others

____ *Verbal:* expressing feelings and concerns

____ *Responsibility:* recognizing and doing your part

____ *Confidence:* feeling able to perform in any situation

_____ *Courage:* inner strength/acting rightly in spite of fear

_____ *Loving:* caring deeply for others

_____ *Problem Solving:* putting your knowledge and ability to use

_____ *Integrity:* telling the truth/living out your convictions

_____ *Determination:* pressing on even when you don't want to

_____ *Creativity:* coming up with new ways to say and do something

_____ *Patience:* being willing to wait

Now take your three most controlling *negative* traits from your list on pages 21–22, and list them alongside the three most desired *positive* qualities from pages 46–47 which you *do not* feel you currently exhibit.

Negative   **Positive**

_____   _____

_____   _____

_____   _____

Now, select a single trait and make a simple decision to change; then act on it. That's how you gain control of your life and become the person God created you to be—a little at a time, a day at a time.

You are created in the image of God, the Master Director. Therefore, you have the ability to think, create, and choose. Within you is the power to decide to adapt your character to the Director's "big picture" view of your life. And a good way to initiate this change is to daily repeat positive affirmations—dialogue that is not intended to be spoken aloud, but to yourself. This inner dialogue is simply an aid to train and discipline your changing character.

Having cut the problem down to a manageable size, create for yourself a "Blueprint Declaration." The brain responds best to statements in first person, present tense, like those listed below. Check an affirmation statement that encourages you to change, or write one of your own in the space provided.

_____ "I am capable of changing my behavior and I choose to do so. I see encouraging progress in my performance each day."

_____ "I refuse to yield to bad habits or destructive thoughts. Minute by minute, day by day, I am accomplishing lasting change."

_____ "I take the initiative to take control of my life. I will not submit myself to anyone, except God, the Master Director. His vision of my performance is the goal, the highest aspiration of my life."

_____ "I no longer let myself be pushed around by past conditioning, circumstances, or other people's expectations. I take time to consider the stage directions provided for me in God's Word and daily strive to improve my performance."

_____ "I always think things through, make a decision, then follow through, knowing that the Master Director is guiding my daily performance, just beyond the footlights."

Write out your own "Blueprint Declaration."

The Light of Consistency

There is one thing you can improve better than anyone else—yourself. One person who stands out in
that effort is Helen Keller. Deaf, blind, and mute, her
early childhood memories were no doubt a series of
shadowy, soundless moments that surely repeated
overwhelming themes of fear and loneliness. Her life
was indeed a dark, disheveled room—that is, until
she discovered the liberating notion that *everything
has a name and that every name has a meaning.*

By comparison, your life is perhaps not as compli-
cated as Helen's but your search for answers may
seem just as dark. However, in your personal quest
for self-understanding, there *is* hope, once you examine your life in the bright light of consistency. In that
moment of illumination you will discover that

> *Everything is a memory, and every memory
> has a meaning.*

But, as the next chapter reveals, the meaning in our
memories can only be interpreted through our individual, personal perceptions.

*There is one thing
you can improve
better than anyone
else—yourself.*

Stage Direction #2: Faith

If diligence is the vehicle that helps you reach an intended goal, then faith is the fuel that makes diligence "go." Faith displays the positive attitude that no matter what the circumstances, the goal *will* be reached.

Faith is more than opinion. It is more than intuition and confidence. It is a rare combination of hope, assurance, inspiration, and trust, fused together with a driving resolve. In essence, faith is simply the ability to see the completion of a thing, even though it has yet to appear. It is our invisible means of support.

In today's tangible, push-button world, society tends to assume that if you can't see it, touch it, taste it, or verify it, then there is no logical reason to believe in it. But if that were altogether true, the space program would never have gotten off the ground.

If Wernher von Braun had not believed the abstract notion that a machine "set on fire" could reach the stars, Neil Armstrong never would have walked on the surface of the moon. Indeed, it took a measure of faith on the part of both of these men to trust in the invisible in order to bring about the improbable. Their intangible faith had a lasting effect on *every* world that mankind will *ever* touch.

Still, in the simple, ordinary adventures of our everyday lives, most of us tend to believe more in the negative probabilities of our circumstances than in the positive possibilities of faith. For instance, you may feel that your childhood recollections and the often negative experiences they hold will in some way "affect" you. That notion is entirely possible. However, the *kind* of effect this flood of memories will have on your future, is totally up to you. Remember, the Bible says, "Faith is the substance of things *hoped for.*"

What do you want to accomplish with your memory journey? Do you believe that it is possible to reach your goal? You can either allow your memories to become a bottomless pit of despair, or you can use them to cross that chasm to the better life that's waiting for you on the other side. With a healthy dose of diligence, you can take a bold step toward your goal by simply allowing your feet to rest on that invisible means of support, that sturdy bridge called faith.

One fellow who allowed himself to take that bold step was a young reporter called Norman.

On a day that began as routine as any other, Norman found himself assigned to his first full-scale catastrophe. Apparently a leaky gas line had flooded a multi-story apartment complex and somehow ignited, blowing away a large section of the occupied building.

Standing behind a police barricade, Norman shaded his face from the heat and watched in horror as many of the panicked residents chose to jump rather than be consumed by the roaring flames. Trying to maintain his composure amid the confusion of sirens and screams, the young reporter flipped open his dog-eared steno pad and began to write. Yet, just as his smoke-filled eyes attempted to focus on his scribbling, a single voice broke through the flames and caught the reporter's ear.

"Please somebody help me! Come and get me! Somebody, hurry, please!"

You can either allow your memories to become a bottomless pit of despair, or you can use them to cross that chasm to the better life that's waiting. . . .

Hearing the desperate cry, Norman's gaze turned upward, and he scanned the building until he pinpointed the small figure of a frantic young girl. She was perched vicariously along the wall of the building's most devastated section.

"Please I can't get down. Somebody help me."

"Listen to me!" a man called out from a window close by. "I can't get to you, Mary. This board won't support both of us. But you can come to me."

The board the man spoke of was nothing but a plank, which had haphazardly fallen across the alley between the rubbled apartments and a neighboring building. "All you have to do," he explained, "is crawl out on the board. C'mon!"

The anxious reporter could see the man's outstretched arms motioning to the young girl, but she wouldn't budge.

"I can't. I'll fall! Please somebody come get me!"

As Norman watched, now oblivious to his pad and pen, a section of debris broke loose and fell with a crash, dangerously near to the stranded youngster. Instantly and without consciously thinking, the reporter tossed the tools of his trade to a bystander and jumped the police barricade. Fixing his eyes on the young girl, Norman zigzagged his way through the maze of scurrying firemen until he reached the closest possible location to the child.

"Please," the girl screamed across to the helpless man in the window, "come get me!"

"Don't look down, just listen." Norman cupped his hands to his mouth and shouted. "There's no one over there who can help you, Mary. But there is someone with you who can!"

"There's nobody up here," the girl whimpered, looking down at Norman.

"Yes, there is, Mary," the reporter reassured. "God is up there with you. He's holding out His hand. He won't let you fall!"

"I'm scared! I can't move! I can't!"

"Yes, you can! God's waiting to help you, but you've got to work with Him. *He* put that board there for you. He *meant* for you to use it."

Clinging desperately to the shaky wall, the youngster remained immobile and continued to cry.

"Mary, believe me," Norman called out in earnest. "God is there with you. He told you so Himself. He said, 'I am with you *always*.' That means *now!*" As the reporter confidently spoke, Mary's ridged, frightened body slowly relaxed and began to move.

"That's it, you're doing fine," he coached. "Now, crawl out on the board. The bridge God provided. It's good, strong, and plenty wide."

Grasping the board, feeling its weight and thickness, the youngster froze once again. "I can't!"

"Think Mary, think! If that board was on the ground, you could cross it with your eyes shut. So do it! Close your eyes and go!"

Gradually, to the point of slow motion, the young girl edged out onto the board, her eyes shut tight. The plank creaked and bowed under her weight, but the wooden span refused to buckle.

Cupping his hands to his face again, Norman shouted. "Just keep saying to yourself, *'With God's help I can do it. With God's help I am doing it. God and I are doing it!'*"

Suspended high above the alley, her trembling voice began to repeat each line. "With God's help I can do it. With God's help I *am* doing it!" Inching slowly but surely across the breach, her voice grew stronger. "God and I *are* doing it!"

Finally, as Norman peered up through the smoky haze, a pair of strong arms appeared in the window and took hold of the young girl.

"You did it, Mary!" The young reporter leaped and shouted. "You and God did it!"

After basking a moment in the joy of the rescue, Norman gathered himself. Remembering his assignment, he made his way back to the police barricade to retrieve his pad and pen. There, the bystander patted him on back and smiled. "Hey, nice goin' out there. You're some preacher!" Quickly turning to face the man, the young reporter shook his head and scowled, "I'm not a preacher."

Shrugging his shoulders the bystander raised an eyebrow and countered, "Well, you should be, mister. You sure should be."

The man's words echoed in the reporter's ears for weeks, conjuring painful memories of his childhood days as a rebellious pastor's son. In time the young man came to realize that *the child he once was, still remained*. And illuminated by the light of that consistency, he could no longer deny the true nature of his character; he knew that the smiling bystander was right.

Eventually, young Norman Vincent Peale summoned up his measure of faith, and doing so he changed the course of his own story. That day he laid down his pad and pen, picked up a Bible, and whispered to himself the words he had shouted up to the frightened youngster, the words he knew for certain would see him through: *With God's help I can do it.*

Whether it be a frightened child's journey across a dangerous chasm, Armstrong's trek to the surface of the moon, or your voyage into the secrets of your childhood memories, the one common ingredient necessary to ensure a positive outcome is the attribute of faith. It is more than opinion. It is more than intuition. It is even more than confidence. It is a rare combination of hope, assurance, inspiration, and trust, fused together with a diligent, driving resolve.

Your personal quest to unlock the secrets of your childhood memories may seem as scary as traversing a shaky wooden plank. But remember, the attribute of faith is your invisible means of support. It is the ability to concentrate more on what you can do to a situation, than what the situation can do to you.

If you will follow your stage directions and acquire this necessary attribute, you, like Wernher von Braun, can have a tangible effect on every world you touch. Like the young girl, you can make it across the chasm of doubts to that better life that's waiting. And like Norman, you can actually change the course of your story.

Be *diligent,* and have *faith* for positive results, for as Peter the fisherman guaranteed, "If you do these things, you will never fall."

Chapter Three

Personal Perspective

*"God hath given you one face,
and you make yourselves another."*
—Hamlet

By now you've learned that everything you have ever seen, smelled, tasted, heard, or felt is filed away in that vast storehouse called your brain. This incredible video-library, situated between your ears, has a memory capacity far superior to the most sophisticated computer. Every glaring act, every subtle detail of your life is there in your head, recorded in vivid, high-resolution, 3-D, sensoround Technicolor. But in contrast to an actor on stage, the camera is not on you . . . you are the camera.

Your filed-away memories are recorded from *your* point of view. Every scene is displayed from *your* perspective. Right about now you may be wondering, "If every memory is stored in my head, why don't I remember *everything*?" Once again, the Law of Creative Consistency is at work. Your individual perception selects only those memories that fit—or seem to fit—your present view of yourself. Your memories are the reflections of who you are, how you feel, and how you react today.

Susan's memory is no exception.

When I was two or three, my mother and I were taking a trip on a train. I needed to use the bathroom. When I got there, I noticed there was no bottom to the toilet—it opened straight down to the tracks that were rushing below. My mother tried to put me on the seat, but I wouldn't let her. I kicked and screamed, "No! no!" until she let me go. I was afraid of falling through.

After hearing Susan recount this recollection during a memory exploration seminar, Randy suggested that there might be times when Susan, the adult, feared that the bottom of her life might unexpectedly fall out. A sudden look of denial flashed across her face. For an instant, Randy thought she might walk out of the session.

Later, however, upon giving his assessment some thought, Susan came to Randy and admitted, "I thought this memory analysis stuff was a crock when you said what you did about my memory. But I've been thinking about it, and I guess you're right. You hit me where I hurt, and I couldn't admit it. I actually do fear the bottom of life falling through. My husband has reminded me of several times in the past months when I've been gripped by fear. I now realize that I must work on this area. So, thanks, I really learned something valuable today."

As an adult, we often see ourselves as too mature to scream "No! No!" every time we face a challenging situation. But when those experiences come along, our library of memories instinctively plays back those selective recollections that echo our deepest emotions. And as those scenes of personal perception replay, our current feelings of insecurity and fear are validated.

Your personal perception is what you perceive to be happening. As a child, those perceptions of reality can be deceiving. Your memories can lie to you. And if those childhood thoughts are allowed to cloud your adult view, you will continue to see yourself as you currently do. Solomon said it best: *"For as he thinks in his heart, so is he"* (Prov. 23:7). If you want to move forward with your life, you have to confront what is in your way. If you want to change the present direction of your character, you must put your personal perception in its proper place. And to do that correctly, you, like Susan, have to confront it.

Go back to your Childhood Memories #1, 2, and 3 in chapter 1. Choose one of the scenes to focus on. What makes this memory stand out to you?

Your memories can lie to you.

Through the lens of your personal perception, how has this recollection affected your life?

What is the dominant feeling you associate with this memory *(anger, love, belonging, rejection)*?

What bothers you about this memory?

What would your life be like today if that scene had never taken place?

What can you learn from this memory to alter the future plot of your story?

Can you put this memory aside and move on?

Should you put this memory aside? Why?

Working through this section will help you discover how early memories can indicate patterns in the life script you are acting out. It can help you uncover any lies about life you tell yourself and indicate any faulty perceptions you act upon. Once you are aware of those lies and how they impact your life, you will be able to do something about them. (We will explore this deeper in Part Two.)

We see the world through the distorted lens of our own personal camera. Others may attempt to fog our lens with their insights, but as adults we ultimately determine how we view ourselves and the world around us. How do you see yourself and the world?

Based on your childhood memories, think of two words or phrases to complete the following statements.

I am _____

Other people are _____

The world is _____

The way you view yourself and your surroundings determines your present position and current direction. And as we have already stated, the earlier the

As adults we ultimately determine how we view ourselves and the world around us.

memory the better. Let's go back to your childhood and learn more about how you became the person you are today.

Another way to understand yourself in the light of your personal perspective is to examine the way you perceived how *others* saw you. Let's examine your childhood appearance. For some of you, this exercise may prove to be difficult. Just keep in mind that at one point along the way we have *all experienced* the feeling of being an ugly duckling. And the more thoroughly you explore these past feelings, the more successful you will be at changing your future.

Randy Carlson, for instance, had quite an interesting childhood image. According to his mother's kind description, he was "stocky." His brother Warren, the oldest, was a ham radio operator. Larry, second of the brothers, was a master of the piano. Randy was simply know as "Fat Butt."

While he didn't like being shot at with BB guns or being teased, Randy did find a positive side to his graphic nickname. It at least gave him a sense of belonging. It was a role he could easily fill. As unpleasant as it sounded, that label stuck with him all through his chubby childhood, not just because it fit the perception that Warren and Larry had of Randy, but also because it fit Randy's view of himself.

His perception of how others viewed his appearance caused Randy to often feel the pangs of insecurity, which he abated with constant eating. "Food," Randy admits, "was a silent partner in my battle to belong." To put it simply, Randy's posterior often made him feel inferior. All puns aside, can *you* relate to Randy's childhood experience?

What was your appearance like as a child? Describe yourself with as much detail and emotion as possible (i.e., tall, skinny, short, fat, unattractive, pretty).

Were you different from your peers (i.e., ears stuck out, overweight, big nose, etc.)?

Did your peers comment about your appearance?

Describe their treatment of you.

How did you respond to their comments?

How did you feel about their treatment of you?

Describe your earliest awareness of your physical difference.

How has your appearance changed over the years? One fellow found that the rest of him grew to fit his nose and today he is quite "normal" looking. Childhood plumpness can give way to a youthful athletic build. Be specific as to how you have changed since your early memories.

How have these childhood memories affected your current view of yourself? Describe the negative or positive influences these memories have had on your personal perspective.

I am/am not (circle one) over these childhood memories. (Sign your first name to the statement true of yourself.)

These memories assist me in recognizing where I once was, so that I can be stronger as an adult. I do not condemn myself.

These memories are still somewhat painful. There is no need to reject who I am, but I'm still struggling.

Perhaps your childhood memories regarding your appearance are all favorable. Describe how others viewed your positive self-image.

Now focus on your present self-image in light of these childhood recollections. Do you see any improvement or are you too critical of yourself? Keep in mind the concepts of condemnation and conviction.

Congratulations! You have just taken a serious look at yourself—and survived! You have accomplished a task that many find difficult: you have taken the first step in confronting your own personality face-to-face. That's quite an accomplishment. You are now well on your way to unlocking the secrets that can bring about a serious change in your life's story.

Typecasting

Now let's take your self-exploration a step further. We have rewound your memory and glimpsed not only the way you perceive yourself but also the way *you think* others perceive you. Now let's examine the *real you;* the true, visible character that *others actually see* on a daily basis.

Study the following character types carefully. As you read through the ingredients of each personality, consider the traits that truthfully describe your individual character, and highlight them.

Controllers

They see the world as a serious place. Much of their energy is spent on keeping other people in line with their own expectations. Controllers have precise definitions of right and wrong and expect those under their authority to toe the line.

A controller says:

- "*I am* going to do things my way."
- "*Other people are* not to be trusted to do things as well as I can."
- "*The world is* a mess and it needs to be set right—that is, with my help."

Controllers expect those under their authority to toe the line.

Two Types of Controllers

OFFENSIVE	DEFENSIVE
• Act upon life and the people around them. They enjoy making things happen and often create chaos	• Govern out of a fear of being dominated or crushed
• Enjoy competition	• Hard to function without being in charge

OFFENSIVE	DEFENSIVE
• Make things happen	• High expectations of others
• Have a temper	• Have tempers
• Wish other people would take life more seriously	• Do not enjoy surprises
	• Prefer to work alone

Drivers

Drivers do not usually complete workbooks! *(Except for drivers driven to unlock the secrets of their childhood memories.)* They do not have the time. The clock tends to be the chief adversary of their life.

A driver says:

- "*I am* goal-oriented and will do whatever it takes to reach my objective."
- "*Other people are* obstructions who will interfere with the reaching of my goals, if I let them."
- "*The world is* full of things to be done."

Qualities of a Driver

- Works from a daily checklist
- Has to complete the daily checklist
- Feels that reaching goals is more important than spending time with people
- Prefers to win
- Childhood memories center around successes and accomplishments
- Can hardly sit still
- Task-oriented rather than people-oriented
- The job comes first

A driver says "I am goal-oriented and will do whatever it takes to reach my objective."

Rationalizers

These intellectuals will do almost anything to avoid emotions. They like lofty talk. Do not expect them to get too friendly.

A rationalizer says:

- "*I am* quite content within myself, for there is nothing coming my way I cannot handle."
- "*Other people are* responsible for their own actions and I leave them to their own little world."
- "*The world is* quite in need of intellectual change brought about by better education and training of the individual."

Qualities of a Rationalizer

- Gives an appearance of "having it all together"
- Never directly looks people in the eye
- May leave the attitude that he or she is better than others
- Feels very vulnerable inside
- Has few social skills
- Speaks in highly educational, lofty terms so as to stay distant
- Tries never to admit or reveal personal emotions
- May speak down to people who are less educated
- Tends to rely upon intellect
- Does not let people get close

Pleasers

Pleasers work diligently and relentlessly to accommodate their perpetual need to please.

A rationalizer says, "Other people are responsible for their own actions and I leave them to their own little world."

The pleaser says:

- "*I am* trying but I never quite do enough."
- "*Other people are* relying on me to do a little bit more."
- "*The world is* full of people I am responsible to make happy, and if I don't, they won't like me."

The pleaser says, "The world is full of people I am responsible to make happy, and if I don't, they won't like me."

Basic Qualities of a Pleaser

- Has poor self-esteem
- Lacks confidence
- Always tries to keep the peace
- Has feelings of never getting anything right
- Feels overpowered by own children and/or family
- Is unable to say no
- Gives in easily, yet desires to run own life

Victims

They often trip through the curtain and fall into the spotlight of center stage. Victims are disasters looking for a place to happen.

The victim says:

- "*I am* surely the most unfortunate of human beings."
- "*Other people are* going to have to take pity and make allowances for my plight."
- "*The world is* surely out to get me, and it is succeeding!"

Qualities of a Victim

- Seeks sympathy or pity from others
- Uses words such as me, my, and I followed by a list of complaints

- Talks in terms of, "Did I tell you about my last operation?"
- Lists aches and pains as if they were the daily menu items
- Likes to be the center of attention
- Feels like others are taking advantage of him or her
- May think in terms of "the world is out to get me"
- Early childhood may center around illness or suffering

Victims are disasters looking for a place to happen.

Are you still highlighting characteristics that describe you? Is this exercise becoming a little too painful? Would it help you to know that these character types are not you but merely tendencies you have developed? It is time to be honest and learn how to adapt. Remember, you cannot change your character, but you *can* strengthen your weaknesses and learn how to avoid the "trait traps" of your personality. Knowledge is power. Learn, grow, adapt.

Let's continue. Remember, you are highlighting the traits that truthfully describe your character.

Martyrs

Martyrs are often substance abusers who are out of work but continue to play the lottery in hopes of someday making it big.

The martyr says:

- "*I am* someone who needs to suffer—by putting myself out."
- "*Other people are* to be helped and served."
- "*The world is* unfair, but I don't deserve anything better anyway."

The martyr says, "I am someone who needs to suffer—by putting myself out."

Qualities of a Martyr

- Serves beyond normal limits
- Sacrifices self and perhaps family for others
- Does not allow others to give to or serve him or her
- Takes blame when no blame is necessary
- Waits on Ed McMahon to bring the next million dollars to the doorstep
- Does not succeed in work because of negative thinking: "I'll just fail again"
- Sets others up to reject him or her
- Rejects self
- Tries to cause the dependence of others

Charmers

Charmers clown their way through every scene to the delight of their ever-present audience. These characters live to make people laugh. They are master entertainers, skillful at beguiling their public. They are comfortable at center stage and pout if they do not get their way.

The charmer says:

- "*I am* here and all is right with the world!"
- "*Other people are* my adoring public."
- "*The world is* my stage and I hope I can hold its attention."

Qualities of Charmer

- Sometimes is seen as being silly
- Steals the show wherever the show is located
- Is like a clown on the outside but feels rejected on the inside
- Thrives in making people laugh

- Is too busy to get close to people
- Remembers the "good times"
- Has few or no real deep relationships with friends
- Can hardly stay still long enough to realize what responsibility is all about

Now go back and review all of the highlights for each character quality. Was there one that seemed to describe you 100 percent? Did you come in way ahead in one category? Did you tie in two or get rather close in a couple of descriptions? Complete the following statements.

From this initial investigation, my onstage character most resembles the traits of _____.

Two or three descriptions I can relate to are

The charmer says, "The world is my stage and I hope I can hold its attention."

Now write your own descriptions of each character type.

Controllers act like _____

Drivers go through life like _____

Rationalizers use their intellects rather than _____

Pleasers respond to others by _____

Victims think _____

Martyrs expect _____

Charmers respond to life like _____

Which character type most resembles your early childhood view of yourself? _____

According to the traits you highlighted, which character type best fits you now?

I seem to be a _____

Do you struggle with any of these roles? Can you see yourself as a character who exhibits one of these tendencies? Explain.

Based upon the definitions given above, draw a truthful, no-holds-barred portrait of yourself illustrating the tendency(ies) that best describes you: for instance, a Goody-Goody who always seeks to please everyone and tires from trying without succeeding, or a Controller who walks around with his/her finger outstretched telling everyone how to change.

This exercise will help you see yourself in a different yet more concrete way.

Title Role: _____.

(Controller, Rationalizer, etc.)

Draw your character here.

Study your work of art. Did you choose the right character for yourself? How does the illustrated image compare to the way you *thought* you saw yourself?

What three traits would those around you say you need to change?

1. _____

2. _____

3. _____

Compare your answers to your list of positive traits in chapter 2.

Any similarities?

Your past is the road map for your future, but only you have the power to change your course. While you cannot recast your character, you can reroute the direction your character is headed. However, to accomplish all this will take more than just a passing notion and a spurt of energy. Remember, the only place you will ever see the word *success* come before the word *work* . . . is in the dictionary.

Your past is the road map for your future.

"In all labor there is profit,/But mere talk leads only to poverty" (Prov. 14:23 NASB).

So far, you have discovered the subconscious consistencies of your character. You have set the stage and explored the singular human nature of your personality, from both your own point of view and that of others. Reflecting on these findings, what *secrets* have you unlocked so far? Describe them below (such as, *I am a Controller who tries to run the world. I am a Charmer who keeps looking for life's spotlight. I feel I should change my pride for humility*).

Based on these new discoveries, re-answer the following statements.

My character is _____.

Other players are _____.

The world stage is _____.

Personal Motivation

For every action, there is an equal (and often opposite) reaction. Although this definition is usually applied to the elementary laws of Science 101, it is a vivid description of Human Nature 101 as well. In the study of humanity, it is called *motivation.*

A nervous young performer once asked entertainer George Burns how he determined the proper motivation for a role. The old, cigar-chomping vaudevillian squinted up at the newcomer and replied, "Kid, it's easy—you knock on a door and if a voice on the other side says, 'Come in,' you turn the knob, open the door, and step through."

What Burns was telling the young man was simply: *Motivation isn't acting but rather reacting to the reactions of others.*

Motivation is the incentive that makes you do what you do. It is your individual response to the environment surrounding you. For instance, if someone compliments your work or appearance, a common response would be a pleasant smile or shy blush. On the other hand, if your efforts are bluntly reprimanded or your appearance ridiculed, your reactions could vary from a raging physical or verbal counterattack to total humiliation and a hasty exit.

Like an actor onstage, your life's performance is constantly influenced by the atmosphere, the events, and the people who surround you. These ever-present factors, viewed through your personal perception, dictate your response—*not just in the one scene in which they originally occurred, but in every scene forever after.*

Your reactions, whether good or bad, right or wrong, are the combined results of every reaction you have ever displayed, from childhood to this very instant. Viewed through the creative consistency of your personal perception, your unconscious mind remembers every detail of every scene. These recollections are appraised by your permanent personality. Then, using these evaluations—in conjunction with the current circumstances—your character instantly devises your present-day reaction.

In effect, you are "programmed" from childhood to react to your present problems just as you have *always* responded. *The child you once were, you still are.*

In an effort to understand why you are motivated in a particular way, and to achieve a change in those responses, you must examine the development of your earliest motivations. To understand why you consistently do what you do, you must explore your *past personal perceptions* of those people and events which you have reacted to up until now.

By studying your view of the atmosphere and characters who first appeared on your stage, you will gain a better understanding of your own personal motivations. In the next section we will begin that study at the most logical starting point: at the beginning, with your home and family.

You are "programmed" from childhood to react to your present problems just as you have always responded.

Stage Direction #3: Virtue

Virtue is developed in conjunction with the realignment of your personal perspective. Being virtuous begins with an increase of moral strength, and ultimately results in your character being endowed with a measure of perceived authority and confidence. For instance, when a couple are joined in marriage, the ceremony is concluded with the words, "By *virtue* of the *power* vested in me, I now pronounce you, man and wife."

The minister or justice of the peace officiating at the ceremony is given the lawful authority to say these words, either by his church or by the state government. He is saying, in essence, "Because of the *confidence* and *respect* certain authorities have in me, I now possess the power, or ability, to join you together to form a new family."

The same principle applies when you acquire virtue. This third attribute on Peter's list of stage directions provides your personal perspective with the God-given confidence, the individual sense of credibility, to believe you are worthy of a second chance: "By virtue of the supreme confidence God has vested in me, I now grant myself the opportunity to improve." By virtue of this realigned personal perspective, you can actually re-form your character.

In the context of your memory journey, virtue gives you the ability to rise above your constant self-defeating notions, evaluate your true worth, and get on with your life. But it is important to note that no one—not the church, not the state, not even your next-door neighbor—can give you that all-important sense of self-worth. The self-respecting confidence of virtue is a privilege only you can grant yourself. Or, as Shakespeare said, "Our remedies oft in ourselves do lie."

Perhaps you recall seeing the movie *The Wizard of Oz*. In that colorful tale, each of the characters was searching for one special thing they thought they lacked. The Scarecrow wanted a brain. The Tin Man desired a heart. The Lion longed for courage. And Dorothy simply wanted to go home and be reunited with her family. At the end of their eventful, witch-hunting adventure, they finally found a fellow who possessed the self-confidence to call himself The Wizard. This man ultimately opened their eyes to the one and only thing that was lacking in their individual characters.

The Scarecrow, though frightened of fire, longed to possess the means to decipher its volatile makeup and devise new and inventive uses for it. To this fellow who yearned for the ability to think, the Wizard explained:

"Anybody can have a brain. Every creature that crawls on the earth, or slinks through slimy seas has a brain. Back where I come from we have universities, seats of great learning, where men go to become great thinkers. And when they come out, they think deep thoughts—and with no more brains than you have. But they have one thing you haven't got: a diploma. Therefore, [he handed the Scarecrow a rolled-up document of sheepskin] *by virtue of the authority vested in me by the universitatis-committeeatum-e-pluribus-unum, I hereby confer upon you the honorary degree of THD. That's doctor of thinkology."*

The diploma that the Wizard conjured up was as "genuine" as the "universitatis" he made up. However, his contrivance was not intended as a ruse, but rather as a reason, a legitimate excuse for the Scarecrow to *think about* the virtue resident in his natural abilities. And doing so, he gained the confidence necessary to recognize the mental capacity he *already possessed*.

Next came the Lion. His problem was a common one. Franklin Roosevelt once said, "The only thing we have to fear is fear itself," which pretty much sums up the Lion's seeming lack of virtue. By all appearances this king of the jungle was afraid of his fear—of fear.

Putting his arm around the cowering cat, "the Wizard observed:

"You are a victim of disorganized thinking. You are under the unfortunate delusion that simply because you run away from danger, you have no courage. You are confusing courage with confidence. Back where I come from, we have people who are called heroes. Once a year they take their fortitude out of mothballs and parade it down the main street of the city. And they have no more courage than you have. But they have one thing you haven't got: a medal. Therefore, for meritorious conduct, extraordinary valor, conspicuous bravery against wicked witches, I award you the Triplecross. You are now a member of the Legion of Courage."

The Lion's medal was nothing more than an excuse to recognize the self-confidence he unconsciously harbored within his furry frame. It was the Wizard's way of providing the Lion with a justifiable reason to look within himself and acknowledge his true nature. And when he did so, his newfound self-respect prompted an immediate, courageous change in his character.

The Tin Man's situation is all too familiar. He perceived himself to be inferior to everyone around him. Because he was made of tin, he thought he was incapable of feeling. In fact, he considered himself to be so inadequate at dealing with life's ever-changing sensitivities that he tended to rust to the point of immobility at the first sign of rain. To this seemingly unfeeling character, the Wizard confided:

> *"Hearts will never be practical until they can be made unbreakable. Back where I come from there are feeling people who do nothing all day but good deeds. They are called, er, eh, good-deed-doers. And their hearts are no bigger than yours. But they have one thing you haven't got: a testimonial. Therefore, in consideration of your kindness, I take pleasure in presenting you with a small token of our esteem and affection."*

As the Wizard handed the teary eyed Tin Man a heart-shaped trinket, he added, *"Remember my sentimental friend, that a heart is not judged by how much you love, but by how much you are loved by others."*

Like the Scarecrow and Lion before him, the Tin Man's trinket did not possess the power to grant him the virtue he sought. However, as before, the Wizard's testimonial simply provided the Tin Man with a reason to *feel* for himself. And doing so he acknowledged that special part of his character which he had unconsciously allowed to rust.

When it finally came to Dorothy, it took more than the Wizard's wisdom to get her to recognize her own self-worth. Like most humans, she had to be convinced that she could actually go home again. Because of her lack of confidence in herself, Dorothy didn't think she would ever be reunited with her family. That uniquely human quirk of self-debasement is a prison most cruel and claustrophobic.

It took the spectacular arrival of Glenda the Good Witch to ultimately open her eyes. Pointing to Dorothy's ruby slippers, Glenda revealed, *"You don't need to be helped. You have always had the power to go back to Kansas."*

Suddenly Dorothy saw herself and her situation in a whole new light. By virtue of her newfound knowledge, she finally recognized the power she possessed, the reprieve she had long sought for from her self-imposed captivity. In that moment of enlightenment she gained a healthy new respect for herself, and with it, the necessary virtue to propel her all the way back home.

The power of virtue is a privilege that only you can grant to yourself. Nevertheless, to assimilate this attribute into your personality, you must first apply the two previous attributes of diligence and faith to your character. In your quest to improve yourself, you must remember that *the grain in the wood of your character is already set*. And only by persistent diligence and faith can you muster the authority to veto its lifelong jurisdiction over your personality.

If you have the faith to believe you can alter your life and you possess the daily diligence to maintain those changes, then you have already attained a measure of self-confidence. And if you work at preserving that high standard, then you will soon begin to see things from a different perspective. Eventually, you will discover that you've been endowed with the authority, the self-respecting nature of virtue.

The fact that you are alive gives you value. By virtue of your birth and existence you have the right to life, liberty, and the pursuit of happiness. Like the Scarecrow, the Lion, and the Tin Man, you, too, can rise above your self-defeating notions. If you will simply evaluate your inherent abilities and recognize your true worth, you can get on with the task of improving yourself without any doubt.

A wise man said it this way, "It is far more important that one's life should be perceived than that it should be transformed; for no sooner than it has been perceived, than it transforms itself of its own accord."

To one degree or another, we all share Dorothy's lack of confidence in finding our way back home. But with a diligent evaluating attitude, and the invisible support of faith, we can each click our heels together and declare, "By virtue of the confidence and respect I have vested in myself, I now grant my character the opportunity to improve."

Virtue is not something you discover somewhere over the rainbow; it is the qualities of confidence and respect you must ultimately find within yourself.

Chapter Four

Casting the Family

"Parents can only give a child roots and wings."
—*Chinese Proverb*

In the last chapter, we explored your personal perception. Now let's look at the early atmosphere, events, and people that helped shape your unique view.

In our book, we refer to your parents as "the kingpin and queenpin of your family theater troupe." Your parents set the initial stage. They created the set and provided the props for your debut performance. And in the context of that unique atmosphere, each member of your family portrayed a specific character. Your memories began on the family stage.

As you ad-libbed your way through those early scenes, you quickly learned through trial and error what would work for you and what would not. Your responses to your family troupe's improvisations helped carve the grain of your permanent personal-

Your memories began on the family stage.

ity. In short, the school that prepared you for the world stage was an acting class called *home*.

Every home has an atmosphere and your residence was no exception. However, the composite of one's domestic climate solely depends upon the characters who populate it. And in the context of your childhood memories, your early home atmosphere was inhabited and mainly influenced by your parents.

Although we know generalizations can be dangerous, research has shown that individuals with similar personalities and problems tend to come from similar family atmospheres. This is as true for those who come from encouraging, nurturing families as it is for those who have grown up in critical and abusive environments.

To see the way family atmospheres connect with memory exploration and how they affect your present-day character, let's compare your childhood memories with the emotional climates defined in *Unlocking the Secrets of Your Childhood Memories*.

First, let's identify the prominent atmospheres found in the home. Study the definitions below. Consider how one or more of these climates influenced your early home life. Put a check mark next to the climate(s) that best depicts your childhood home.

____ Authoritarian

In this environment, the parents—especially the father—rule the house. The conditions of such a home often reflect a seriousness about life that demands a "roll call" followed by lecture and obedience to the day's commands. Discipline is often swift and not always deserved. This kind of family is motivated primarily by fear.

___ Perfectionistic

This home reflects the white-glove look of a flawless family. The home climate may range from mere impeccability to "absolute" perfection. Not only are things tidy and in their places, but the children and pets are poised and ready for *Better Homes and Gardens* magazine to arrive at any moment.

___ Permissive

Words like *compromise* and *no self-discipline* describe this atmosphere. This home goes through life from one event to another with little plan or perception of change. In contrast to authoritarian households, the children rule the parents in this family.

___ Martyristic

This household feels like "The System" is always out to get them. Living in such a negative climate compels the inhabitants to live by the "glass is half empty" standard. This family speaks of the Great Depression as if it ended only last week. Each family member would gleefully walk five miles to the market and back—uphill—just so they could complain about it. Such folks are reminiscent of the Addams Family at a beautiful flower show—terribly depressed and loving it.

___ Competitive

This is the classic residence of stage mothers and overzealous athletic-coach fathers. The interior of such a home may resemble the scene of a Broadway audition and/or an Olympic qualifying meet. The members of this family are constantly on the go, striving to keep up with the Joneses.

_____ Neglectful

In contrast to the competitive family, the parents of this group care very little for their children because they are usually preoccupied with their own concerns. Such parents may not be abusive, but rather, they are irresponsible. Often one or more members of the family are drug and/or alcohol users. This type of household is trapped in a vicious circle of selfishness.

_____ Materialistic

The members of this household are the ultimate control freaks. They must possess the reins of power at all costs. They are constantly striving to acquire money, influence, and the upper hand. (This group sounds more like the U.S. House of Representatives than the typical all-American home.) Their slogan is, "The one with the most toys wins."

_____ Hurried

The most prized possession in this household is the clock. The children of this family are forced to grow up fast. It seems that there is never enough time to stop and smell the pizza. This type of family can never find a moment to stop and get to know one another.

Now go back and <u>underline</u> the climates that you feel are _currently present in your home._

You have identified the basic climate(s) that comprised your early surroundings. And you have recognized the similarities in your current home. Are these similarities merely coincidental? Unlikely. As we have already learned, you are motivated by your environment. _(For every action there is a reaction.)_ Your personal atmosphere is influenced by the people who inhabit it. And in the context of your childhood memories, the inhabitants who influenced you the most, early on, were your parents.

Your mother and father created the set and provided the props for your initial performances. Your early responses to their reactions are what shaped the grain of your present character. Therefore, to examine the similarities between your past and present self, we must explore your past and present perceptions of Mom and Dad.

Let's begin with your father.

Mary's childhood view of her dad conjured up feelings of security, strength, and love. And as the years passed, the lessons she unconsciously learned from his strong example had a definite impact on the grain of her present-day character. It is no coincidence that her current family atmosphere is similar to the climate of her childhood. And her fondest memory of her father is a poignant example of that consistency.

Your early responses to [your parents'] reactions are what shaped the grain of your present character.

It was the Christmas of my college sophomore year, and I recall that my father was going through one of the most difficult periods of his life. The situation had taken such a toll on him that he resigned his job. He and Mom were forced to move to the little lake cottage Dad had built for our summer vacations.

We always had our big family around on Christmas, with everything as warm and fuzzy as you can imagine; but that year it was different. My sister had just married and she was spending the holiday with her new husband's family. And my grandparents were gone. When I arrived at the cabin that year, it was just Mom, Dad, and me.

I remember that as we went about the task of trying to be cheerful for one another, Daddy asked me, *"Would you like to help me cut down the tree this year?"* Of course, he knew what my answer would be. So we got on our boots, our coats, and our hats, and trudged out into the knee-high Michigan snow.

As Dad sawed down the tree we chose, I recall watching the slump of his shoulders. I could clearly see that the weight of the world was on him. In no time, the small tree fell. Dad reached to pick up the trunk's heavy end, and I, instinctively, bent down and took hold of the tree's point.

At that moment, it was as if everything shifted—and I knew it. Suddenly, I realized that I was not a child. I was an adult. It was time for me to pick up *my end* of my family's grown-up responsibilities. I realized that this man who had put so many good things in my life now needed me to do the same for him.

I remember that as we walked back through the snow to the cabin, everything seemed different. *I* was the grown-up now, and my father was the one who needed to be nurtured and cared for.

During that memorable Christmas with Dad, I came to realize that I was no longer the only one who required support and understanding. Instead, I was a participant in a ceremony, celebrating a childhood that I could no longer afford . . . I was a grown-up now.

Mary's perception of her father was positive. And that respectable view had a generous impact in shaping her perception of herself. In contrast to Mary's memory, let's examine the earliest recollection of a man everyone in the world knows:

> I remember being beaten by my father. I remember vowing to myself never to cry again. So I stood there silently, counting the blows as my father beat my body.

The negative, unfeeling view this youngster had of his father worked its way into the grain of his developing personality. It shaped the personal perception of not only himself but also his view of the world at large. That simple, stoic childhood memory was the foundation for the brutal, sadistic, power-hungry character of Adolf Hitler.

We've seen the diverse ways in which the personal perception of one's father can shape a life. Now let's take a closer look at *your* personal view of your dad.

My earliest memory of how I was parented by my father:

My next earliest memory of how I was parented by my father:

On your early life stage, what kind of character did your father play? Complete the following.

At times I found my father to be the hero I needed. He was like a hero to me because he

Did your "hero" (father) always wear white? List some human faults even heroic fathers have.

At times I found my father to be a villain. He was like a villain to me because he

Even villains sometimes wear black and white plaid, even gray. (They don't always wear blatant black.) Are there strong points or good memories that you might also remember? List some of the strong or good points that even villains possess.

Perhaps your father portrayed more of a "supporting role" and never assumed the lead. He may have been absent from the home, or present in the home yet without definite character definition. If his role in your life was just a "bit part," explain how that affected you and why you believe he chose to remain in the background.

What character qualities can you identify in his life?

At times my dad was:

(circle all that apply)

Authoritarian

Permissive

Competitive

Materialistic

Perfectionistic

Martyristic

Neglectful

Hurried

Check the statement that most honestly reflects how you feel toward your father at this very moment:

_____ I want to be like my father.

_____ I'll never be like my father.

During this exercise you may have flashed on scenes of being the child of a cruel father. If that's what you remember, don't fight it. Let those memories and the feelings they stir escape. You have held them in too long. Don't deny your feelings.

Denial is a subconscious mechanism that seeks to protect you from emotions you fear will somehow lead to destruction. You may be afraid to face the pain of your past, afraid you might drown in your tears, or worse, conclude that the wound your father inflicted cannot be healed. But denying the existence of the wound will not keep it from festering, and it certainly won't encourage recovery.

Denying the existence of the wound will not keep it from festering.

If you have ignored, overlooked, or in some fashion dismissed certain portions of your father memories, then you are experiencing a degree of denial. In their book *Forgiveness,* Sidney and Suzanne Simon suggest that you are in a stage of denial if you find yourself thinking that old injuries and injustices are

- unimportant
- water under the bridge
- irrelevant to your life today
- not worth dredging up again
- over and done with
- better off forgotten

By contrast, the Simons suggest that people who are willing to confront the hurts they've been hiding from themselves, often use "non-denial" statements.

Check the declarations below about your father memories which you have recently thought to yourself, or told someone aloud:

_____ "I was hurt."

_____ "What happened to me still hurts."

_____ "That was no way to treat me."

_____ "It was wrong."

_____ "I have suffered because of what I went through."

_____ "I haven't gotten over it yet."

_____ "It *was* that bad."

But . . .

_____ "I can talk about the experience without self-destruction."

_____ "I do not have to shut down my feelings or push things out of my mind to survive."

_____ "God accepts me just as I am, with the past I can't change."

_____ "I can live with a clean, honest, acceptance of my past."

If you hesitate in checking any of the statements above, remember there is someone you can trust, just beyond the footlights of your stage. God, the Master Director, is always there waiting to advise and guide you. All you need to do is ask: *"If any of you lacks wisdom, let him ask of God, who gives to all liberally and without reproach, and it will be given to him"* (James 1:5).

Now, keeping in mind these things, let's move on and consider your mother and her influence on your life.

For the most part, the mother is the nurturer of the family. In most cases she is the parent children relate to the most. Although the old typecast roles of "working father" and "homemaker mom" have faded, it is still safe to say that there is a special "closeness" between mother and child. After all, we spend the first nine months of our life surrounded by our mother. She is the portal through which each of us enters the world.

However, no matter what role your mother has played in your life, there is no denying that she remains a major influence in the development of your character. The person you are today can be attributed to the perceptions you had of her during *your childhood*.

Take Heather, for example. This twenty-eight year-old mother of three youngsters had come for counseling because of her overwhelming feeling of anger with others—especially her children. She felt guilty, confused, and afraid that her pent-up rage might explode and harm the kids.

Assessing the situation, Randy Carlson spent several hours with her on mother/daughter issues that needed to be resolved. Those sessions eventually led Heather to a series of three revealing childhood memories about her mother . . . and herself.

When I was a kid, I did more listening than talking. I remember one day my friend Joan was telling me about her parents' divorce when my mother came into the bedroom where we were and made Joan go home. I was really mad at my mother for doing that when Joan needed to talk to me. I told my mother how I felt—but she didn't listen. She never did. . . .

. . . I must have been six or seven at the time, and I recall that my grandmother was very ill. She was living in our spare bedroom. One day when everybody was gone except for Grandma and me, she had one of her attacks and couldn't get to the bathroom to get her medicine. She yelled downstairs for help and I remember going up and getting the medicine for her and sitting with her for about an hour before the attack passed. It felt good to help my grandmother when she needed help. . . .

. . . I remember that my mother and I fought a lot. She never tried to understand me or listen to me. I recall one day that my friend Joan had to move out of state. I was crying and feeling pretty sorry about the whole thing when my mother came in and told me to stop crying, grow up, and get out into the kitchen and get the dishes washed. I was furious and felt really hurt that she didn't try to understand how I was feeling about Joan's leaving.

In these three early scenes from Heather's life, Randy pieced together the jigsaw puzzle of her present-day adult personality. "Even though so much of your focus is wrapped up in the anger and the conflict between you and your mother," Carlson explained to Heather, "I see in your memories a person who really cares about other people, someone who is willing to listen to their problems, and wants to help others and care for them. And that's a pretty positive picture in my book."

Heather realized her need to change her focus from anger to healthy, positive attitudes. Together, she and Randy Carlson found those positive attributes hidden in her early memories of angry exchanges with Mom.

- She is willing to stand up for what is right. (In her first memory, Heather says, "I told my mother how I felt.")
- She feels strongly about issues. ("I felt really sad that Joan was moving.")
- She needs and enjoys lasting relationships. (The entire third memory concerns her sense of her loss when her friend moved.)

Heather discovered how her early memories of Mom influenced her personal character. Now let's see how your mother influenced you. Complete the sentences below.

My earliest memory of how I was parented by my mother:

My next earliest memory of how I was parented by my mother:

On the stage of your early life, what kind of character did your mother play? Complete the following.

At times I found my mother to be the heroine I needed. She was like a heroine to me because she

Did your "heroine" (mother) always wear white? List some normal human faults even heroic mothers have.

Even female villains sometimes wear calico. (They don't always wear black either.) Are there strong points or good memories that you might also remember? List some of the strong or good points that she possessed.

At times, I found my mother to be a villain. She was like a villain to me because she

Perhaps your mother portrayed more of a "supporting role" and never assumed the lead. If her role in your life was just a "bit part," explain how that affected you and why you believe she chose to remain in the background.

What character qualities can you identify in her life?

At times my mom was

(circle all that apply)

Authoritarian

Permissive

Competitive

Materialistic

Perfectionistic

Martyristic

Neglectful

Hurried

Check the statement that most honestly reflects how you feel toward your mother at this very moment.

_____ I want to be like my mother.

_____ I'll never be like my mother.

Perhaps you recall being the child of an unloving mother. If so, as we have stated before, don't fight those memories. No matter how negative those scenes may be, let go of those recollections and their attached feelings. Let them escape. You have held them in too long. Don't deny your feelings.

If you have ignored, overlooked, or in some fashion dismissed certain portions of your mother memories, then you are experiencing a degree of denial. If you feel that you cannot get past these locked emotions, review your earliest memory of how you were parented by your mother on page 100.

Remember, like the youngster learning to ride a bike, you, too, may feel as though you are wobbling and about to fall. Nevertheless, there is someone you can trust running alongside, keeping an ever watchful eye on your progress. God is always there for you. He is ready and willing to guide you. All you need to do is call:

"Whoever calls on the name of the Lord/Shall be saved" (Joel 2:32).

The Big Picture

We have defined the prominent atmospheres that influenced your childhood home, and we have examined how your parents fit into those early scenes of your life. Now let's put those two elements together and look at the big picture. Let's see how they have affected not only your individual character but also the home you have made for yourself today.

Am I the product of an *authoritarian family*?

Growing up in an Authoritarian home can lead children to become adults who display certain aspects of the same character. Place a check by those statements that best describe you.

_____ I tend to be inconsiderate of others.

_____ I tend to be quarrelsome.

_____ I am unpopular.

_____ I need to work on being a better listener.

_____ I am sensitive to blame.

_____ I do not know what to do when I am praised.

_____ I consider myself to be polite but shy.

_____ I consider myself to be respectful but timid.

_____ I rebelled in later life when I was free of authority.

_____ I have trouble resolving my own problems without the help of authority.

_____ I am not the most resourceful person.

_____ I am not spontaneous.

_____ I find that I stretch the truth (lie) at times.

_____ I find that I take (steal) things not belonging to me.

Look back at your check marks. Is it possible that you are somewhat a product of an authoritarian home influence?

I have a memory of the authority in my home. At the age of _____, I remember a time when

Am I the product of a *perfectionistic household*?

Growing up in a perfectionistic home can lead children to become adults who display certain aspects of the same character. Place a check beside the statements that best describe you today.

_____ I feel like I never measure up.

_____ I could do better.

_____ I do have low self-esteem.

_____ I feel like a failure.

_____ I am most critical of myself.

_____ I make mistakes, but I will get even with myself for doing so.

_____ I often lash out against myself, even for the slightest error or mistake.

_____ I say yes to too many projects.

_____ I put things off if there is not enough time to get it "done right away."

Look back at your check marks. Is it possible that you have been influenced by a perfectionistic home atmosphere?

I have a memory of the perfectionism in my home. At the age of _____, I remember a time when

Am I the product of a *permissive family?*

Growing up in a permissive home can lead children to become adults who display certain aspects of the same character. Those reared in an overly permissive family tend to also have specific identifiable qualities. Place a check beside the statements that best describe you today.

_____ I find myself with few true friends.

_____ I have a somewhat compulsive behavior.

_____ I overspend.

_____ I overeat.

_____ I am tempted to overdrink.

_____ I find self-control to be absent in my life.

_____ I seem to have a lack of consideration for others.

_____ I can be quick to speak without caring what others might feel as a result.

_____ I want what I want now (inability to delay gratification).

Look back at your check marks. Is it possible that you have been influenced by a permissive home atmosphere?

I have a memory of the permissiveness in my home. At the age of _____, I remember a time when

Am I the product of a *martyr atmosphere?*

Growing up in a martyr climate can lead children to become adults who display certain aspects of the same character. Can you relate to any of the characteristics common to those raised in such a family? Place a check beside the statements that best describe you today.

_____ I don't think life has much to offer me.

_____ I pride myself in not breaking any of the Ten Commandments . . . at least in the past ten minutes.

_____ I feel somewhat self-righteous toward others.

_____ I can become most judgmental at times.

_____ I find I control others through guilt.

_____ I do try to manipulate those around me.

Look back at your check marks. Is it possible that you have been influenced by a martyr atmosphere?

I have a memory of martyrdom in my home. At the age of _____, I remember a time when

Am I the product of a *competitive family?*

Growing up in a climate of competition can lead children to become adults who display certain aspects of the same character. Do you feel any of the characteristics common to those raised in such a family? Place a check beside the statements that best describe you today.

_____ I always feel a need to succeed.

_____ I must do more.

_____ I cannot let the neighbors next door outshine me in anything.

_____ I will climb the ladder to success as soon as possible.

_____ I must look my best at all times.

_____ I feel like second best is not good enough.

_____ I do not like to lose.

_____ I don't care how you play the game as long as you win.

_____ I never settle for second best.

_____ I am driven.

_____ I find my work becoming increasingly important to me.

Look back at your check marks. Is it possible that you have been influenced by a competitive home atmosphere?

I have a memory of competition in my home. At the age of _____, I remember a time when

Am I the product of a *neglectful family*?

Growing up in a neglectful climate can lead children to become adults who display certain aspects of the same character. Do you feel any of the characteristics common to those raised in such a family? Place a check beside the statements that best describe you today.

_____ I do not remember following a set daily schedule.

_____ Special time for family activities was never carried out.

_____ I am often prone to depression.

_____ Daily responsibilities can seem overwhelming.

_____ I tend to live from moment-to-moment.

_____ I am forgetful.

_____ I feel like we hardly have time for one another.

_____ I feel unimportant.

_____ I never had a sense of responsibility while growing up.

_____ I do not want to grow old.

Look back at your check marks. Is it possible that you have been influenced by a neglectful home atmosphere?

I have a memory of neglect in my home. At the age of _____, I remember a time when

Am I the product of a *materialistic family?*

Growing up in a materialistic climate can lead children to become adults who display certain aspects of the same character. Do you feel any of the characteristics common to those raised in such a family? Place a check beside the statements that best describe you today.

_____ I sometimes feel like I have too many things.

_____ Caring for many things is beginning to bother me.

_____ I want the latest model, style, or fashion, even if I already have something similar.

_____ Activities take away from family time.

_____ I feel like I am always on the go.

_____ I never have time for me.

_____ I seem never to have time for others.

_____ Sometimes I feel guilty about my standard of living when I see others who are less fortunate.

_____ I am given to depression.

_____ I buy more and enjoy it less.

Look back at your check marks. Is it possible that you have been influenced by a materialistic home atmosphere?

I have a memory of materialism in my home. At the age of _____, I remember a time when

Am I the product of a *hurried family?*

Growing up in a hurried climate can lead children to become adults who display certain aspects of the same character. Do you feel any of the characteristics common to those raised in such a family? Place a check beside the statements that best describe you today.

_____ I find myself always on the go.

_____ I feel a need to excel.

_____ I did not like getting any grades lower than "A" when I was in school.

_____ I don't have many intimate relationships.

_____ I am prone to being a bit tired.

_____ I seem to never have time to sit still.

_____ I feel like I am behind in my responsibilities.

_____ I feel driven to improve.

_____ I feel like life is short and I must make the most of it.

Look back at your check marks. Is it possible that you have been influenced by a hurried home atmosphere?

I have a memory of being too hurried. At the age of _____, I remember a time when

Review the check marks you've made on pages 104–112. Then check one or more of the following climates from which you came.

_____ Authoritarian

_____ Perfectionistic

_____ Permissive

_____ Martyristic

_____ Competitive

_____ Neglectful

_____ Materialistic

_____ Hurried

Look back at the memories you recorded that reflected your home atmosphere. How much were you affected by the environment? (Circle one.)

None   Little   Considerably   Lots   Totally

Mark the description from chapter 3 that best fits your parents, with the letter *D* for Dad, *M* for Mom, and *B* for both.

_____ **Controllers:** Cannot let go. (Codependency)

_____ **Drivers:** Finish and succeed or bust. (Compulsive)

_____ **Rationalizers:** Reasons or explains away everything so as to avoid direct responsibility and all emotions (feelings). (Avoidance Issues)

_____ **Pleasers/Goody Two-Shoes:** Tries harder. (Obsessive)

_____ **Victims:** May not have proper boundaries in place. (Assertive Issues)

_____ **Martyrs:** Always needs a cause. (Self-Image Problems)

_____ **Charmers/Getters:** Must always be in the spotlight. (Vain Tendencies)

Draw a "theater poster" of your family in a way that displays these tendencies. For instance, controllers walk around with their finger pointed at you, telling you how to change. What is the title of the play your picture is advertising?

(The Controller(s), The Rationalizer(s), The Controlling Rationalizers, etc.)

What does this picture tell you about your family atmosphere?

Your Place on the Stage

You may ask yourself, Where do I fit into this picture? That question can easily be answered by asking another more involved question: In relationship to your brothers and sisters, where do you fit into the chronological order of birth?

The order of your arrival in your family is another factor that influences who you are today. There are four birth order categories: only child, firstborn, the middle child, and the last born or baby. Before we go on, let's answer that basic first question: Where do you fit in your family's birth order? Circle the correct answer.

I am: firstborn only child middle last born/baby

Each one of these categories possesses characteristics that affect the way in which you responded to your immediate family as well as how you react to your world today. And your early childhood memories reflect those unique characteristics.

The order of your arrival in your family is another factor that influences who you are today.

First or Only Child	Middle Child	Last Born or Baby
Early childhood memories are likely to reflect:	Early childhood memories are likely to reflect:	Early childhood memories are likely to reflect:
<ul><li>Times of special achievement</li><li>Being bothered by mistakes</li><li>Being the "good" child</li><li>Concern about the approval of others</li><li>A need to do things right</li><li>Detailed work</li><li>Stress, loneliness, fear</li><li>A need to show older kids "I can do that"</li></ul>	<ul><li>Feelings of not belonging</li><li>Having lots of friends</li><li>Feeling sensitive about being treated unjustly</li><li>Being a good negotiator</li></ul>	<ul><li>Getting the attention of others</li><li>Being cute</li><li>Celebrations, receiving gifts</li><li>Having others do things for you because you were too little</li><li>Dislike of being the "littlest" or baby</li></ul>

Thumb back through the earliest memories you have described in this workbook and draw a star by those memories that were influenced by your birth order. Find at least two key memories that were a direct result of birth order.

Your memories began on your family stage. As you play your role, you discover by trial and error what works for you and what does not. Based on what you have learned so far, let's do a little more sketching.

Draw a stage in the space provided. On this stage we are going to do what is called "blocking a scene." This theatrical term means that we are going to assign a specific spot on the stage for each of the actors in your family troupe. The placement of each character is going to be according to birth order. Don't forget to include yourself!

Downstage—Near the front of the stage, in the main spotlight draw the *firstborn or only child.* Place him/her inside the circle of the spotlight, center stage.

Upstage—Center and further away from the audience, closer to the back of the stage, draw the *middle child.* Although not as easily visible in the footlights, he/she constantly acts as the intermediary, the negotiator for the rest of the family troupe.

Downstage—Stepping into the circle of the spotlight, in front of all the others, draw the *last born, or baby*—the scene stealer.

If this sketch has left you feeling a bit confused, you may be a firstborn who acts more like a middle child, but there are usually good reasons for that. One important birth order rule says that *any gap of five years or more between children starts the entire system over again.* For example, firstborn male . . . four-year gap . . . second-born male . . . six-year gap . . . third-born male.

What is the time gap between you and your nearest older sibling? _____

What is the time gap between you and your nearest younger sibling? _____

You may remember that Randy Carlson has two older brothers, one six years and the other ten years his senior. Randy was the last born in his family, but instead of reflecting the characteristics of the baby, he exhibits the organizational, cautious, and serious traits of a firstborn or only child. He would never think of coming to work without a coat and tie, while Kevin Leman often shows up wearing tennis shoes, shorts, and a sports shirt.

Do you feel that the time gap between your older and younger siblings has affected the standard definition of *your* birth order? _____ If so, answer the following.

I am a . . .   Firstborn   Middle born   Last born/Baby

The time gap between my birth and my nearest sibling(s) tends to place me in the class of a . . .

Firstborn   Middle born   Last born/Baby

Describe an early memory that demonstrates your answer(s) to the previous exercise.

Now, in the space provided, illustrate the scene you just described by placing yourself on the platform according to the birth order answer you gave.

Another factor in your childhood climate and early development is the birth order of your parents. If two perfectionistic "firstborns" get together, they are going to raise their children differently than two "babies" would.

Keeping in mind the possible time-gap influence of their siblings, complete the following phrases by circling the best answer.

My father is: Firstborn   Only child   Middle   Last born
My mother is: Firstborn   Only child   Middle   Last born

Birth order, however, is just a part of your personality puzzle. The more pieces you find that fit, the better you will be able to understand yourself. Kevin Leman puts it this way, "Childhood memories are even more reliable than birth order as an indicator of why you are the way you are, since these memories are the tapes you play in your head, which determine your response to everyday living."

"Childhood memories are even more reliable than birth order as an indicator of why you are the way you are."
—Dr. Kevin Leman

Part One Review

Now let's examine what you have learned so far.

Overall, I feel that my childhood was . . . (draw a stick figure of yourself at the appropriate place on the scale.)

0   1   2   3   4   5   6   7   8   9   10
—Terrible —   — Average —   — Wonderful —

I rate my childhood as I do because of one particular early incident. Describe that memory.

What emotion(s) do you attach to that memory?

In my memories I often felt:

As an adult I often feel:

In my memories . . .

I am _____

Other people are _____

The world is _____

Today I feel that . . .

I am _____

Other people are _____

The world is _____

I have discovered that my positive traits are

I have also discovered that my negative traits are

My present-day character was influenced by parents who were

_____ Controllers

_____ Drivers

_____ Rationalizers

_____ Pleasers

_____ Victims

_____ Martyrs

_____ Charmers

My present-day character was affected by the atmosphere of my childhood home, which was predominantly:

_____ Authoritarian

_____ Perfectionistic

_____ Permissive

_____ Martyristic

_____ Competitive

_____ Neglectful

_____ Materialistic

_____ Hurried

My memories of being _____bring to mind
(birth order)

positive/negative emotions.
   (circle one)

What part of this workbook has been most enlightening to you so far?

How has this study begun to change your view of your childhood memories?

How has this study begun to change your present-day view of life?

Complete the following statements by filling in the blanks.

As the lead in this play of life, I strive to

Without my part, this story would be

I am thankful for my role, for it expresses

I accept my role in the play of life, because

Now list the questions you still have about your present life and personal character.

Take these questions with you as you begin Part Two.

If all the world is truly a stage and we, the men and women of this world, are the players—then we are the ones who are in control.

It is your actions and reactions that shape the course of the play. Your surroundings do not affect the scenes of your life. It is rather your *personal perception* of those surroundings that actually influences the direction of your individual plot. Therefore, you have the ability within you to change the course of your story.

You have made the first move in that effort. You have taken a step back and looked at yourself through the viewfinder of your childhood memories. You have faced the mistakes of your past and begun to understand the true nature of your character. But you still have a ways to go.

You have the ability within you to change the course of your story.

The ability to change your story is within you, but to use that tool effectively takes strength. Remember, knowledge is power; the more you have the stronger you are. In fact, the Bible says that "wisdom is better than strength" (Eccl. 9:16). To alter your life's story requires more than just knowing the mistakes of the past, you must also possess the knowledge of how to avoid those inbred character flaws and adapt yourself accordingly. That is the next step in your memory exploration.

You have set the stage. Now let's move on to Part Two, where you will discover the secret of how *you* can change the story.

Stage Direction #4: Knowledge

Although the majority of today's world tends to believe that when graduation day is over, so is the need for learning, nothing could be farther from the truth. From the moment you are born, until the day you take your last breath, you are "in school." Everything you touch, smell, taste, see, and hear is filed away into that vast storehouse called your brain. This accumulation of knowledge absorbs itself into the pores of your personality and helps to shape the character you ultimate become. To put it simply, you are what you **learn.**

The word *knowledge* in the context of Peter's list implies "practical wisdom." It is information gathered from books and teachers and put into practice. If your character already possesses the *diligence* to seek wisdom, the *faith* to believe that it can be found, and the *virtue,* the enabling "confidence," to learn, then the often time-consuming responsibility of acquiring *knowledge* can indeed turn into an enjoyable adventure. If you never aspire to gain the proper knowledge, you will never have control over your life, or what is permanently filed away into your personal mental "storehouse."

In the context of your memory journey knowledge is mandatory. It is vital that you *know* which of your recollections are important. You must be able to *comprehend* their lessons, *assimilate* and *evaluate* the data, and *apply* the information to the development of your character. Acquiring the attribute of knowledge is, in effect, the process of learning how to use the tools of wisdom in the affairs of everyday life.

The tools of wisdom are three separate, yet combined forces that work together in close harmony with the emotional, psychological, and physical components of the human personality: *Sophia, Phronesis,* and *Sunesis;* or, cleverness, common sense, and insight (putting two and two together). The use of these tools noticeably enhances a character's onstage performance.

Sophia

Sophia is a Greek word for "skill, cleverness, and learning." This form of understanding influences the emotional, the driven, side of our intellect. It deals particularly with the gift of extraordinary insight. Sophia allows us to comprehend new ideas, create and implement new concepts, and gain a special understanding of life's "Big Picture." It is that spark of ad-lib genius that understands the ultimate goal of our life play and cleverly devises the means to attain it.

A good example of sophia can be found in the wisdom of Abraham Lincoln. Faced with the possibility of a dissolved Union and the overthrow of his government, President Lincoln acted and reacted to overcome his adverse circumstances with an uncanny sense of innovation. He was uniquely aware of his ultimate goal and the creative means necessary to accomplish it. *"My oath,"* Lincoln once wrote to a friend, *"imposed upon me the duty of preserving, by every indispensable means, that government—that nation—of which that Constitution was the organic law. Was it possible to lose the nation, and yet preserve the Constitution?*

"By general law, life and limb must be protected; yet often the limb must be amputated to save a life; but a life is never wisely given to save a limb. I felt that measures, otherwise unconstitutional, might

*become lawful, by becoming indispensable to the preservation of the Constitution."**

Lincoln knew that his ultimate purpose was to salvage the nation and safeguard its principles. However, his sophia intuition, communicating with his emotional, inspired side enabled him to see that accomplishing this feat would require a great deal of creative, unorthodox action.

What "limbs" did the President have to amputate to save the life of the Union? Actually, none. However, he did creatively twist a few arms in order to fulfill his ultimate goal: For instance his decision to resupply Fort Sumter, rather than evacuate or initiate hostilities, turned out to be a shrewdly calculated move. Not only was it consistent with his "big picture" strategy of holding on, it was a tactic of inspired stubbornness which eventually forced the impatient Confederates to fire on the fort and begin the Civil War, thus providing the North with a reason to support Lincoln's future actions.

In short, Lincoln saw a way to make the South fire the first shot. When they did so, he used that aggressive act to garner the support of his constituency. Taking advantage of that support and its timing, he seized the initiative and took the reigns of his weighing government in hand. That shrewd succession of chess moves set the stage for Lincoln's unparalleled presidency. And in the hindsight of history, it initiated the ultimate plot change in America's story.

Through his cultivated insight of sophia, Abraham Lincoln was made constantly aware of the most cur-

From the moment you are born until the day you take your last breath, you are "in school."

---

*All reference to Abraham Lincoln quotes are from *Lincoln on Leadership*, Donald T. Phillips (New York: Warner Books, 1992).

rent, efficient ways to fulfill his ultimate goal. Though Lincoln was an incredible man, his capacity for inspired knowledge was no greater than yours. The same insightful qualities that once took up residence in the Civil War White House can also reside within you.

Once you have developed a keen sensitivity to the instincts of sophia, your ultimate goal will come into clearer focus. You will be able to see clearly, as Peter put it, *"afar off"* and possess the ability to recognize the proper chess moves that will facilitate your success.

If sophia reveals the footpath to your ultimate goal, then phronesis tells you the proper shoes to wear for the journey. It is the wisdom of small details.

Phronesis

The second facet of knowledge is *phronesis*. In the Greek, this word denotes "common sense understanding and practical knowledge." This facet of wisdom directs its influence toward our rational, psychological mind, making us aware of the practical, ordinary things that shape our daily lives.

This important part of knowledge does not concern itself with the "Big Picture"; instead, it focuses on the subtle shades, the colors and brush strokes that fill the picture frame. Phronesis is the ability to recognize life's small problems and understand just how to handle them so that they do not grow into major difficulties.

The most common of these potentially inflatable problems is mishandled interpersonal relationships. The way you act and react toward others may not seem significant at the moment, but like an unattended match, such overlooked incidents of insensitivity have a way of bursting into a destructive flame.

Again, a good illustration of this tool in action is the life of America's sixteenth president, Abraham Lincoln.

On the whole, Abe was not thrilled with the pushy, know-it-all people who constantly cornered him to discuss how *they would* run the war. Yet instead of harshly turning away such individuals, Lincoln's sense of phronesis-discretion had a way of easing them out of his path, often by using a subtle, but effective anecdote. On one such occasion when a delegation of angry, demanding politicians invaded his office, Lincoln shrewdly shut them off by saying, *"Gentlemen, suppose all the property you were worth was in gold and this you had placed in the hands of [one man] to carry across the Niagara River on a rope. Would you shake the cable and keep shouting at him, 'Stand up a little straighter; stoop a little more; go a little faster, go a little slower, lean more to the south'? No, you would hold your breath, as well as your tongue, and keep your hands off until he got safely over. This Government is carrying an enormous weight. Untold treasure is in (its) hands. Don't bother them. Keep silent and we will get you safely across."*

Lincoln knew just what to say and how to say it in order to keep his little problem, little. Had he flown off the handle and ordered them all out of his office, he would have certainly been able to clear the room; but in accomplishing that momentary goal, he would have alienated the very men necessary to accomplish his ultimate purpose. Therefore, his developed sense of phronesis (the ability to recognize the small details of a situation), guided him to appeal to the politicians' selfish perspective. Doing so with a smile and a pat on the back, he was able to get them to immediately leave with not only a better understanding of *his* point of view, but also with a more amiable opinion of Lincoln himself.

On the stage of your daily life, this trait of phronesis-knowledge will help you to evaluate each scene to better understand the subtle dangers and conflicts that plague your ad-libbed moments. Once you have developed its instincts, like Lincoln, you will be able to sense those small, but possible dangers which always hide in the shadows. You will be able to better ad-lib the right words and the proper actions. And you will know better how to change the course of potentially unsalvageable situations.

This facet of wisdom is also a valuable asset in the exploration of your memories. If sophia helps you to see down the road to the ultimate goal of your life, then phronesis will help you to notice the small details along the way—those potholes, oil slicks, and patches of broken glass that can unexpectedly slow you or bring you to an abrupt halt.

Sunesis

The third facet of knowledge is *sunesis*, "understanding, insight, a running together" (or as we would say today, "putting two and two together"). This function of wisdom utilizes the five senses of the body as information collectors. It instantaneously scans that vast storehouse of "filed-away knowledge" inside your head, extrapolates the necessary facts and designs a plan of action, tailor-made to fit your unique set of circumstances. And the sum of this "two plus two" formula affects the decisions you will ultimately make and the development of your character.

If little Johnny is told to "take out the trash" and he fails to do so, his father is then forced to teach him the importance of obedience through punishment. Whether it takes the form of revoked privileges or a spanking, the boy soon learns that if the garbage is not removed, either his rights or the sense of feeling in his backside will be! One way or another obedience is a lesson he most certainly will "file away."

No doubt when Johnny is faced again with his father and this dirty chore he will compare his stored-up knowledge of that past experience, with his father's intimidating glare. And quickly evaluating the situation in his "sunesis mind," he will decide to pick up the garbage cans and take them out to the street.

Sunesis is indeed a mental tool of great value. It advises its user on the proper ways to handle a given situation by using the combined knowledge of the senses and past "filed away" experiences. Nevertheless, although the instinct of sunesis is advantageous, it is the most effective when its ability is linked with sophia's insight and the practical perspectives of phronesis. Combined, these three tools constitute the purest form of applied knowledge.

Each one of these tools performs a particular function in the construction of a thought. Sophia reveals your ultimate goal and devises the master route to get there. Phronesis checks the path for stumbling blocks and monitors your attitude and rate of speed. And through your five natural senses sunesis (the ability to put two and two together) evaluates all of the incoming information and formulates your final decisions. However, each of these tools is an aspect of knowledge and should not be considered knowledge itself. Only when you combine these tools into one working unit do you truly possess the attribute of knowledge.

Look at it this way: If you have the shell of an egg, you do *not* have an egg. If the whites of an egg are all you possess, you still don't have an egg. Even if you have both the whites and the shell, the "yolks" on you, because you have yet to own a complete egg. However, if you have the whites, the yolk, and the shell *intact*, then and only then do you truly have an egg.

The same is true of knowledge. To possess the full compliment of wisdom, you must acquire all three of its facets. When you have accomplished this and begun to exhibit the characteristics of sophia, phronesis, and sunesis, then and only then will you truly possess the attribute of genuine knowledge.

The accumulation of knowledge absorbs itself into the pores of your personality and helps to shape the character you ultimate become. *You are what you learn.* Therefore, if you never aspire to gain the proper knowledge, you will never have control over your life or what is permanently filed away into your personal mental "storehouse."

What is your ultimate goal? What do you want to accomplish with your memory journey? How do you plan to reach your goal? Are you often unsure of how you should handle potentially "inflatable" situations? Have you ever asked yourself, "Why didn't I see that problem coming?"

All of the questions can be easily answered once you have followed Peter's stage directions and acquired the character trait of knowledge.

Part Two

You Can Change the Story

Chapter Five

Ad-*Just the Facts*

"To thine own self be true."
—William Shakespeare, "Hamlet"

When Sergeant Joe Friday, of the classic TV series "Dragnet," was assigned to a case, he had only one goal in mind: *"Just the facts, Ma'am."* He had the hard job to uncover the truth about events that he did not personally witness.

In contrast to Sgt. Joe, your job is much easier. You already know the facts. You were there when the events in question occurred. Therefore, in your case, you don't need *"just the facts"*—you need to "ad-*just* the facts" that you already have filed away in that vast court transcriber called your brain.

However, like the majority of the witnesses Joe Friday questioned, you either don't always see the event correctly or you'd rather not reveal what you know—even to yourself, for the facts may tend to incriminate you. That's the way most childhood recollections are remembered.

The answers as to why and how you became your present-day character are there, locked away in your head, because *you are your memories*. And the only way to unlock those secrets is to truthfully examine those events in question—and adjust the facts.

On a cool fall afternoon, a solemn-faced father trudged up the side of a manicured hill of grass holding tightly to the hands of his two young sons. Stopping near a small stone marker, the father knelt to one knee and pulled his sons closer. Pointing down to the weathered monument, he whispered, "Guys, this was *my* father, your grandfather. He died when I was a boy, much younger than both of you. It's ironic," the man's voice broke, "my father left me——and now that the divorce is final, I am leaving you."

As the years passed and the two boys grew, each developed a decidedly different view of their father. The older son grew to feel sorry for the man who was left alone as a boy and dealt such a cruel twist of fate as a man. This son ended up befriending and eventually forgiving his father for abandoning him. However, the other brother was not so forgiving.

"Ad-just the facts."

The younger of the two entered adulthood harboring an attitude of indifference. He blatantly went out of his way to stay out of his father's way. And over the years his seemingly deliberate evasions were staged to inflict the maximum measure of hurt upon the man who had deserted his childhood.

When the two brothers finally confronted each other about their contrasting feelings, they discovered that their individual perceptions of their father had originated with that one, single scene in the cemetery. The forgiving son remembered his father to say, *"My*

father left me . . . and, ironically, I have to leave you."
The not-so-forgiving sibling recalled the event a different way. He remembered his father pointing to him and saying, *"My father left me——so now I am going to leave you."*

Such pivotal memories have a way of affecting every facet of every life involved. As illustrated in this story, the reality of what was done and said in that cemetery was set aside in favor of the childhood perceptions of each brother. The older boy, perceiving more of the truth about the situation, suppressed his fear and disappointment by magnifying his secondary feelings of empathy and compassion. Though his feelings lied to him, it was his way of coping. On the other hand the younger boy, unable to fully grasp the pain in his father's voice, only heard the words, not the intended meaning. Therefore, his memory likewise deceived him.

The result of this single yet shared memory was two brothers harboring divergent emotions that were equally exaggerated but in different directions.

Like these brothers, you tend to see your memories through the viewfinder of your personal perception; which, more often than not is clouded by the haze of your emotions. To *adjust the facts* of these events, you must be willing to face yourself and accept the notion that your memories may be lying to you. And the best way to confront those facts is to learn how to prudently talk to yourself.

Whenever you recall early memories, an important tool comes into play—your self-talk. The term *self-talk* has become popular in recent years, but it is simply a euphemism for the belief system that influences the way you think all day long.

You see your memories through the viewfinder of your personal perception.

Self-talk can involve external speech (talking to yourself out loud), but it usually centers in your thoughts. Most people speak aloud at the rate of 150 to 200 words per minute, but research suggests that you can talk privately to yourself by thinking at rates of up to 1,300 words per minute. Your self-talk is a powerful tool and it works according to several basic principles.

Your Thoughts Create Your Emotions

"For as he thinks in his heart, so is he" (Prov. 23:7a).

Describe a time when your thoughts created a specific emotional response (such as, thinking your parents were angry when they were not, or that a sibling did not like you because you broke one of his or her prized possessions).

Your Thoughts Affect Your Behavior

It follows that your thoughts affect your behavior. For example, if you think you are shy, you will behave like a shy person. And if you behave like a wallflower long enough, you'll start believing that you are. *"Well, that's just the way I am, I guess."* If shyness has plagued you all of your life, your early childhood memories will support this unhealthy view of yourself.

What adverse actions have you taken as a result of a passing thought? *(I thought my brother was going to knock down my building blocks, so I knocked his down first.)*

Your Perceptions Affect Your Thoughts

Your life-style begins with your early perception of the world around you. Those first impressions are critical—and lasting. Once you make them, you simply reinforce them over and over, and that's how the grain of your wood is set. Your early perceptions literally set your course for life.

Your early perceptions literally set your course for life.

Kevin once had a teenage client whose earliest perceptions of life overshadowed any later, positive memories. . . . A Vietnamese girl with scars from cigarette burns on her arms, she had been abused as a baby and adopted at age four by an American couple. Her adoptive home was one of the most loving environments any child could possibly ask for, but she had a chip on her shoulder and saw the world as a hostile, hateful place. Those cigarette burns scarred more than her arms.

Describe a time when you thought a particular event was happening, only to later discover you were mistaken *(I saw the blue police lights in my mirror and I started to pull over, but the squad car zoomed past me).*

You Think Irrationally

Don't take this principle personally. Everybody thinks irrationally sometime. We all say things we don't mean, worry about things that aren't even there, do things that don't make sense.

Randy and his wife, Donna, were having a good, old-fashioned argument—the kind both of them knew would end soon, but they both wanted to get all of their points in before it was over. Randy finally realized he was wrong and apologized to Donna for what he had said. But his quick apology caught her off guard, and he could tell by the look on her face that she didn't want to accept it just yet. She said, "Wait a minute, I'm not done being mad yet."

Rationally, Donna knew she should accept Randy's apology and forget the argument. But part of her wanted to argue a little longer. Was it simply a matter of still being angry and not cooled down enough yet? That's part of the answer, but Donna is like anyone else. *The child you once were, you still are.* And that little child usually shows up in times of stress, like an argument with your spouse. Sometimes you don't want to accept the truth. You'd rather cling to what makes sense to that little child within you—even when the adult part of you knows it doesn't make much sense at all.

Detail an occasion when you momentarily took leave of your otherwise rational mind *(The party was going full blast, I saw the lamp shade—and the next thing I knew I was putting it on my head).*

What Do You Tell Yourself?

Self-talk is a normal and an essential part of the thinking process. Unfortunately, we often fill our thoughts with the wrong information. Let's examine some of the thoughts we harbor regarding ourselves. Deep within the recesses of our subconscious are recurring echoes we dredge up from time to time, into our everyday thinking.

In the classic movie "It's a Wonderful Life," the lead character, George Bailey, convinced himself that *"It would be better if I had never been born."* That lie, compounded by recent events in his life, depressed George to such a degree that on Christmas Eve he walked out onto the Bedford Falls bridge and seriously contemplated the notion of jumping. Yet before he could follow through with his plan, an angel named Clarence leaped into the freezing water first. He knew from studying Bailey's early childhood memories that the heroic child George once was still remained.

After George rescued Clarence, the angel showed Bailey the error of his self-talk by taking him back

We often fill our thoughts with the wrong information.

through his life, through his memories. He compelled George to confront the lie "It would be better if I had never been born." And he did so by showing Bailey how dismal life would have been *without* him. When George finally realized how positive his childhood, as well as his life in general, truly was, he discovered that he really did have an incredible, "wonderful life."

Now put yourself in the role of Clarence, and confront the lies in your own self-talk.

Check the following messages you sometimes give yourself.

    _____ I am stupid.

    _____ I will never be able to do it right.

    _____ There I go again.

    _____ What did I expect from myself, anyway? Perfection?

    _____ I'm just not good enough.

Circle the "lies" in this list.

    I must be perfect.
    I must have everyone's love.
    I am only as good as what I do.
    I must have everyone's approval.
    My problems cause my miserable life.
    I am worthless.
    All of my problems are caused by my sins.
    I only count if, . . .

Did you circle them all? If you did, good! They are *all* lies that are subconsciously spoken every day.

Now compose a list of other statements you often tell yourself.

Confronting the lies of your self-talk really *works!*

Kevin Leman, the pesky little kid who decided *the only way he could count* was to be as off-the-wall as possible in order to be funny, was headed nowhere when he finally saw he needed to change. Eventually, Kevin took the little kid he once was, shaped him up, and taught him to get attention in productive, helpful ways that have touched millions of people.

And then there is Randy Carlson, who grew up "keeping his fat butt down," just in case his brothers were lurking about. Randy's self-talk told him that *the only way he could achieve security* was to try to please everyone, never make waves, and *never, never* take risks. He could have faded into the woodwork and gone carefully through life as a victim who never got a break. Instead, he learned to help other victims and became a leader who realized he didn't need everyone's approval to feel comfortable.

Seven Primary Ways Negative Self-Talk Develops

There are seven primary ways negative self-talk develops:

- *Considering details out of context.* For instance, focusing on one time you failed rather than all of the times you have succeeded.
- *Making blanket judgments.* Having once been rejected, you wrongly conclude, "I'll always be rejected."
- *Overestimating how a situation affects you.* Someone accidently fails to shake your hand at a meeting, and you wrongly conclude that he or she is angry with you.
- *Black-and-white thinking.* Another driver will not allow you into the flow of traffic, so you categorize him or her as a "worthless jerk."
- *Exaggerating the negative aspects of a situation.* A coworker makes an innocent remark about you, and you are angry the rest of the day.
- *Condemning yourself to prerequisites to avoid unhappiness.* You decide you will only be happy if . . .
- *Criticizing yourself on the basis of inadequate or improper information.* Because you had a bad initial contact with someone, you believe that your future contacts with that person will always be bad.

Based on the information above, truthfully acknowledge the negative self-talk behavior(s) you are guilty of displaying *("In the past I have made blanket judgments about . . .").*

In the past I have

In the past I have

In the past I have

Remember: You are not stuck with self-defeating behavior. Let's begin breaking your negative self-talk.

What Should *You Tell Yourself?*

If you were to find yourself alone, shut in a dark, dismal room, chances are it wouldn't be long before you began to *feel* dark and dismal too. We human beings are funny that way; we let our surroundings influence our attitudes. For instance, sunshine on my shoulders makes me happy, while rainy days and Mondays always bring me down.

If the things we see, taste, smell, and feel can affect our moods so intensely, is it any wonder that what we hear (audibly and inwardly) also manipulates our behavior? If you are serious about altering your conduct, your onstage performance, it is fundamentally essential that you *immediately* change the dark, dismal things you hear and say.

Our surroundings influence our attitudes.

What should you tell yourself instead? When in doubt of what to say, you can always find just the right words in God's Master Script: "Whatever things are *true,* whatever things are *noble,* whatever things are *just,* whatever things are *pure,* whatever things are *lovely,* whatever things are *of good report,* if there is any *virtue* and if there is anything *praiseworthy—meditate on these things*" (Phil. 4:8 italics added).

In other words, start to think, say, and listen only to those things that are the opposite of negative. *Think positive! Speak positive! Be positive!*

Start by telling yourself the following statements out loud.

- I don't have to be perfect.
- I'm proud of what I did today.
- I am loved.
- I am fun to be around.
- The world is a better place because I am in it.

Write some additional positive self-talk statements.

Rewrite the following negative self-talk statements into positive statements. The first one is done for you.

1. I am stupid.

1. **I am always learning and becoming smarter.**

2. I will never be able to do it right.

2.

3. There I go again!

3.

4. What did I
   expect from
   myself, anyway?   4.

5. I'm just not good   5.
   enough.

Self-Talk: A Positive G.O.A.L.

Herbert knew the importance of positive self-talk. At seventeen, his doctor told him that his young heart had a fatal flaw. The physician warned him of engaging in any excess physical activity, and he estimated the balance of the boy's brief life in months rather than years.

If anyone had a reason to talk negatively, it was Herbert.

However, despite the grim circumstances, this Tennessee youngster made the uncommon decision to look at the brighter side of things. He figured that even if the doctor had overestimated his allotted time, "What would I gain by behavin' poorly?" Therefore, Herbert went on with his life as if nothing was wrong. Instead of taking it easy, he did just the opposite. People would often shake their heads in dismay as they watched him sprint briskly through town, often bolting up three stairs at a time.

Herbert threw himself into his work. He got involved in local politics, became a deacon in his small-town church, and even went turkey hunting in his spare time. He married a schoolteacher from the next town up the road and went on to father three healthy children.

What was Herbert's secret? He was often heard to say, "I have a G.O.A.L. Everyday I *Get Out And Live.*" And that's *exactly* what he did.

Today, fifty-odd years after his passing at the age of thirty (almost twice the age he was when first diagnosed), Herbert Barton Green is still remembered by the local folk of Dayton, Tennessee as one of their most colorful and positive hometown boys. He successfully changed the course of his story by making the goal of his self-talk . . . Get Out And *LIVE!*

Circle your answer to the following questions.

Yes   No   Are you able to say what you want to say without biting your tongue to keep silent?

Yes   No   Do you have problems keeping your emotions in line?

Yes   No   Do the behavior or problems of others easily bug you?

Yes   No   Do you control others with emotional outbursts?

Yes   No   Do you swallow your emotions to keep them deep down inside so that they will not show?

Yes   No   Do you discourage others from showing emotions?

How do you typically respond to the following feelings? Write down your first, second, and/or third response.

Example:

When I feel sadness, I <u>*cry, go to bed, pray*</u> .

When I feel fear, I _____.

When I am worried, I _____.

When I am angry, I _____.

When I feel insecure, I _____.

When I feel joy, I _____.

When I feel affectionate, I _____.

Study your responses to the two previous exercises, then circle the best answer to the following statement.

My life decisions are dictated by my . . . judgments/ emotions.

Just like actors learning their characters, it is time for us to memorize our script.

No matter what my memories may tell me, no matter what my life-style, I am not stuck with self-defeating behavior. The little kid I once was I still am, but I can live happily ever after anyway.

Read the above passage out loud. Now, repeat it once more, as you fill in the blanks below.

No matter what my _____ may tell me,

no matter what my _____, ___ am not stuck
with self-_____ behavior. The _____
I once _____, I _____, but _____ can live
_____ anyway.

Memorize this. It is just two sentences! You can do it! Spend a few minutes working on it until you are comfortable.

The ABC's of Truth Therapy

We have established that we can be deceived not only through the words we say but also by the memories our personal perception displays. We have examined our negative thoughts and found that *the way to change our attitudes is through the use of constructive self-talk*. But to maintain a positive guard against our own self-deceptions, we need to be aware of the "ABC's of Truth Therapy."

Our first and foremost responsibility is to be truthful with ourselves: "To thine own self be true." It makes no sense to live a life founded on and surrounded by lies. What's the point? If you are content to believe the deceptions of your childhood memories, you'll never be able to change your story. And the primary way to achieve that change in direction is to be willing to move *toward* the truth.

If you are content to believe the deceptions of your childhood memories, you'll never be able to change your story.

To change your story, you must be willing to . . .

• *Accept* the fact that your memories can be lying, at least a little bit.
• *Believe* the truth instead of the lies that are ingrained into your life-style.
• *Change* your behavior by using different self-talk.

Describe a memory that you now *accept* that is not based on the full truth.

Write the recollection as you *originally* remember it.

How did this event affect your self-talk?

Believe the truth.

Identify the error: What *really* happened?

Change . . .

How did the truth about this event originally affect you?

How did *accepting* and eventually *believing* the truth about this event *change* you and your self-talk?

Thumb back through all of the memories you have written so far. Take each of those memories through the ABC's of truth therapy. It is possible those recollections from childhood have left you with misperceptions or lies about yourself.

Now once more, let's *adjust the facts* of your self-talk. Fill in the blanks and repeat the following statements aloud.

No matter what my _____ may tell me, no matter what my _____,

I am not _____ with self-_____ behavior.

The little kid I once was I still _____,

but I _____ live happily ever after anyway.

If you will memorize this simple statement, you, like Herbert, will have set a G.O.A.L. You'll be able to Get Out And Live. You will be closer to maintaining a better image of your present-day character and life in general.

Still, there is more to your memory exploration than just having a better self-image. You must also adjust the facts you have retained regarding your parents. If it is important to you to change the course of your story, you must go back through *all* of the scenes of your life and set the record straight. Only when you confront the lie and adjust the facts accordingly, will you be able to Get Out And Live. *Be Positive,* and have a wonderful life.

With that G.O.A.L. in mind, complete Stage Direction #5. Then, let's move on to Chapter Six.

Only when you confront the lie and adjust the facts accordingly, will you be able to Get Out And Live.

Stage Direction #5: Temperance

The attribute of temperance is by far the most difficult to attain, for to acquire this addition to your character, you must be able to overcome your own will. Temperance is self-control. It is the ability to protect yourself *from* yourself, because you are your own worst enemy.

Human beings are a unique species. We are the only brand of earthlings capable of abstract thought, original concepts, and *free will*. Ironically, when we humans are given a choice, we tend to emulate our less cerebral neighbors, the animals. We revert to our first "childhood emotion" of selfishness: "I want what I want when I want it." And in so doing, we behave like beasts.

This animalistic emotion is ingrained into the most rudimentary functions of mankind's character. Yet despite this singular similarity, our power to choose does distinguish us from earth's other species. And that's where temperance comes in.

Temperance is the ability to willfully restrain your own self-will for the "higher" purpose of self-improvement. When an individual attempts to ad-lib his way through life without the guidance of temperance, his onstage performance almost always crumbles into a fragmented rubble of disappointment and confusion. This happens because we always know what we want, but we rarely know what we need.

Temperance provides you with the tolerance to take a step back; the patience to examine your desire from every angle; and the wisdom to prudently choose between "want" and "wait." Yet seldom does the amount of restraint we put into *waiting* match the measure of stamina we put into *wanting*. This lop-sided formula was never better illustrated than in the classic story of Adam and Eve.

By anyone's standards, Adam had it made. He had a great home (the Garden), a good "job," (looking after Eden and its animal residents), and Eve, a companion to share his fulfilling, well-balanced life. Yet with all of these comforts to sustain him, Adam was coaxed into nibbling the fruit of the only tree that was off limits. Simply put, his "wants" outweighed his will and his chance to improve his character bit the dust. Ironically, in this garden paradise, the only thing he seemed to lack was the temperance, the self-control, to take a step back, see the situation for the lure it was, and as Nancy Reagan would put it, just say no! But then again that's always easier *said* than done.

Every player who has ever set foot on the world's stage has encountered this lack of temperance. It has been the main plot of every drama, clear back to those first recorded stories of mankind. At one time or another we have all given over to that selfish inner voice that says, "Go for it, what have you got to lose. You know you want to. Just say yes!"

In those frequent times of seduction, our human nature blinds us to everything but what our ingrained character "wants." To this day, *the basic human nature man once possessed, still remains.* In the midst of passion or fear, our selfishness still rushes to incapacitate our sense of reason. We are seemingly powerless to keep ourselves from the desires of the moment. All too often we conveniently forget the adage, "To thine own self be true."

What it all comes down to is the simple law of displacement: Where there is no temperance, there is temptation.

Describing the disastrous retreat from Moscow in 1801, Caulaincourt, an officer in Napoleon's army, recounted in vivid detail how the soldiers of the Guard wasted away on the snowy plains of Russia. He disclosed how the men, overcome by the cold, fell out of their ranks and lay prostrate in the snow, being too weak or too numb to stand. Once they fell asleep they were dead. To sleep was to die.

Caulaincourt, the Duke of Vicenza, related that on a number of occasions he tried to arouse the men about him who had fallen on the ground. Yelling loudly and shaking them vigorously, he warned them that they would perish; but the drowsiness engendered by the cold was irresistibly strong. To all his fervent pleas the drowsy soldiers were deaf. The only words they uttered were to beg him to go away and let them sleep—and once asleep, they never awoke.

The attribute of temperance is like the voice of Caulaincourt constantly, fervently reminding the sleepy nature of your human character to resist the irresistible. It is that nagging voice you keep hearing inside your head, yelling the warning, "Wake up!" because you may know what you want, but you rarely know for certain what you need.

Every day you are forced to grapple with your ingrained human nature. No matter which way you turn you're constantly faced with tempting gardens, full of thorns. You can regress to humanity's childhood and *want what you want, when you want it*. Or you can take a step back, adjust the facts, and change the course of your character. Remember, you are a unique brand of earthling; you possess the ability to choose.

To win this struggle requires a *diligence* of purpose, a *faith* to believe that you can improve, a *virtuous* strength to overcome your enticements, and the proper knowledge to adjust the facts accordingly. If you daily strive to display these necessary traits, if you are determined to change your story, if you will heed Peter's stage directions and "Wake up," then the attribute of *temperance* will be as easy to reach as any garden variety apple.

Chapter Six

Pardon Your Parents

"Children begin by loving their parents. As they grow older after a time they judge them. Rarely, if ever, do they forgive them."
—Oscar Wilde

Parenthood is the only vocation that does not require a diploma or license. Like life itself, parenting is a task one learns by doing. Its lessons are taught by trial and error. To put it simply, the proper approach to being a parent is not always apparent. Therefore, everyone in the world is raised by imperfect people—and that includes you.

Knowing this, there must come a point along the way, during *your* equally imperfect life, when you forgive the mistakes of those who nurtured you. For if you cannot overlook the reactions of those who have played a role in your growth, you cannot honestly forgive yourself and change your story.

Carrying the painful luggage of your childhood memories is exhausting, unproductive, and self-

There must come a point when you forgive the mistakes of those who nurtured you.

defeating. Instead of continuing to struggle with this unnecessary burden, you can get rid of it by releasing from your debt those who have hurt you. You have the tools to do it. We examined them in the last chapter: Using the ABC's of truth therapy, you can adjust the childhood view you had of your parents and grant them the only license their vocation merits—the human right of imperfection.

One fellow who accomplished this successfully was the famous actor Gene Hackman.

At the young age of thirteen, Gene recalls one afternoon playing in the street with the other kids from the neighborhood. In the course of his boyhood frolic, his eye happened to catch sight of his father driving by in the family car. The older Hackman, seeing the boy, raised his hand as if waving good-bye. And Gene recalls thinking, *I knew that was the last time I would ever see my father.* It was—that is until years later when Gene the adult, the successful actor, sought out his father and confronted him face-to-face.

"How could you do that to us?" Gene chided. *"How could you just up and leave us like that?"* But the elder Hackman refused to discuss the past. He said, *"I'll only talk to you about the present and the future."*

It was a frustrating situation, which could have easily increased Gene's anger and confusion. However, this actor knew enough about his *own* character to take a step back and try to "view" the overall scene from *outside his personal perception.*

Looking back at his childhood memory—not as that thirteen year old, but rather as an adult—he realized the events of the past were not his fault, he was just a child and that his parents were only human. He concluded that the past was just as painful for his father as it was for him.

Somewhere in this process of self-exploration, the younger Hackman was able to grant his father the human right of imperfection. And today, a well-*adjusted* Gene Hackman happily admits, *"I am so glad I changed my memory."*

Gene was able to let go. What about you? In Part One, chapter 4, "Casting the Family," we covered in good detail the relationship you had with your parents. You determined that they used specific styles of parenting and that you built specific memories of them based on their training. Let's take those memories through the ABC's of truth therapy.

Generally, my parents treated me

My relationship with my parents was

Good   Could've been better   Bad   Average   Poor
(circle one choice)

Based on how my parents treated me, the clearest part of my memory deals with

The strongest feeling I attach to this memory is

My second best memory of how my parents raised me is

The clearest part of this memory is

The strongest feeling I attach to this memory is

It is important to try to understand your parents' perspective. Without that discernment, you are boxing shadows on a dimly lit stage. If you are not willing to relate to their point of view, then you'll never connect. Until you are willing to put yourself in your parents' position and play their roles for a moment, your fists of question and rage will continue swinging vainly at the empty air. Shadows never respond.

It is important to try to understand your parents' perspective.

Let's see how much you know about your parents' views. Check the appropriate boxes.

My Father's General View of . . .	Men	Women
Worthy of respect	☐	☐
Artistic	☐	☐
Creative	☐	☐
Emotional	☐	☐
Faithful	☐	☐
Gentle	☐	☐
Intelligent	☐	☐
Leaders	☐	☐
Mechanical	☐	☐

	Men	Women
Logical	☐	☐
Vulnerable	☐	☐
Strong	☐	☐
Competent worker	☐	☐
Home care duties	☐	☐
Romantic	☐	☐

My Mother's General View of . . .

	Men	Women
Worthy of respect	☐	☐
Artistic	☐	☐
Creative	☐	☐
Emotional	☐	☐
Faithful	☐	☐
Gentle	☐	☐
Intelligent	☐	☐
Leaders	☐	☐
Mechanical	☐	☐
Logical	☐	☐
Vulnerable	☐	☐
Strong	☐	☐
Competent worker	☐	☐
Home care duties	☐	☐
Romantic	☐	☐

How difficult was it for you to answer the previous questions about your mother and father?

Now let's see how you answer the same questions.

My General View of . . .	Men	Women
Worthy of respect	☐	☐
Artistic	☐	☐
Creative	☐	☐
Emotional	☐	☐
Faithful	☐	☐
Gentle	☐	☐
Intelligent	☐	☐
Leaders	☐	☐
Mechanical	☐	☐
Logical	☐	☐
Vulnerable	☐	☐
Strong	☐	☐
Competent worker	☐	☐
Home care duties	☐	☐
Romantic	☐	☐

How close were you in agreeing with your parents' views?

How often did you feel the compulsion to change your answer so as not to agree with your mother or father?

Never   Once or Twice   Frequently   Consistently
(circle the best answer)

Do you struggle to reflect the opposite of what your parents think?

Why?

The Beginning of a "Redo" Life

When Sam came in to see Randy, he was struggling with a heavy bundle of pain and regret. His father had been an alcoholic, and when he was drunk, he regularly beat Sam's mother and occasionally Sam and his little sister.

When Sam was nine, he lost both of his parents. His mother was killed in a car accident, and his father died of liver cancer. Through deep sobs of pain, Sam told Randy, *"I never had a day of peace when my dad was alive, and I have never had a day of security after he died. There is so much I'd like to redo in my life."* As Sam told his story, his comment about wanting to redo things made sense. His life had been a series of frustrations and failures: he had gone through three marriages and the rebelliousness of runaway teenagers. He was constantly in and out of alcohol rehabilitation programs. And he gained and lost three jobs in one year.

Now, at the age of fifty-seven, he, like his father, was facing the helplessness of cancer. Sam's future wasn't sure, his past was a mess, and he felt trapped with nowhere to turn. And his early childhood memories reflected the same vivid images of confusion and damaged emotions.

I was always scared to death of my father. I remember the day that I disagreed with him about some stupid thing. I am not even sure what it was anymore. All I can recall was being pushed into my bedroom, beaten, and then locked in my closet for what seemed to be a couple of hours. I was scared that he would come back and beat me some more if I yelled for help, so I just sat there and cried until he unlocked the door and let me out.

Sam is a tragic example of how a person's life can be twisted by parental cruelty and selfishness. As an adult, Sam was stuck and in need of help. So Randy shared with him the steps to truth therapy, especially rewriting the past in the light of new thinking and a changed perspective.

"Tell me something about your father's background," Randy inquired. "What was his childhood like?"

"Well, he grew up in a poor family down in Mississippi. His father died when he was only five, and his mother remarried when my father was about ten. My father used to say that his stepfather would whip him and put him down all the time. My father didn't have much good to say about his own childhood."

"So, your father didn't get a very good start in life either?" Randy observed.

"I guess he didn't."

"In fact, it sounds like your father only repeated on you what he learned from his own stepdad."

"I suppose you're right," Sam questioned, "but what does that have to do with me?"

"It's perspective, Sam; I want you to put your childhood and all the bad things that happened to you in perspective. Try to humanize your parents—make them real people with real problems. Free them from being only a series of childhood memories and bad feelings."

That weekend, Randy gave Sam some homework. He was to spend the next week thinking about and recording some of the real-life battles and problems his parents faced.

Through this simple process, Sam was able to move his parents from the category of abusive failures to being fellow strugglers, real people with real problems. It didn't excuse their behavior, but it did help Sam. He revised his childhood memories of his parents' mistakes by looking at them with the perceptions of a fifty-seven-year-old adult. His mother and father were no longer locked into the perceptions of a small boy who had lived with fear, anger, abuse, and neglect.

What do you know about your parents? What was your father's greatest struggle as a young man? What about your mother? What were her dreams for her family? Like Sam, let's now explore these and other crucial questions about your parents.

Everyone Who Has Ever Lived Had a Past

Gather the following information from speaking directly with your parents. (If that is not possible, talk to their siblings or your own elder siblings.)

If possible, use this exercise as a means to rebuilding any broken lines of communication that currently exist within your family. Discussing these questions with your relatives should develop a healthy climate for open and honest conversation. You may want to begin with just a phone call. But any effort you make to bridge the communication gap is a beginning in itself.

Father

Dad was born ＿＿＿＿＿＿ (month, day, year).

The place of his birth was (city, town) ＿＿＿＿＿＿,

(state) ＿＿＿＿＿＿＿＿＿＿＿＿＿.

The story of Dad's birth:

Dad completed (years in school) _____. His education prepared him for a career as a _____. Nevertheless, Dad's most enduring talent was/is

Dad met Mom in (year) _____. They were married in (year) _____, after dating for _____. (Tell their story here.)

My father's biological children are:

Dad's toughest personal struggle was:

Mother

Mom was born _____ (month, day, year).
The place of her birth was (city, town) _____,
(state) _____.

The story of Mom's birth:

Mom completed (years in school) ____. Her education
prepared her for a career as a _____. Yet Mom's
most enduring talent was/is

My mother's biological children are:

My mother's toughest personal struggle was:

My parent's life together can be illustrated by the following story:

Using a few brief sentences, fill in the following list.

Happy Times They Shared   **Sad Times They Shared**

Study the facts you have compiled. What insight does this information reveal to you about your parents? *(I now understand and better appreciate their struggles, hopes, fears, and dreams.)* Describe your insights in as much detail as possible.

Read the following questions carefully and fill in the blanks.

As a Child . . .
Who in your family did you compare yourself to?

_____

Who in your family did you contrast the most?

_____

Who enjoyed *you?* _____

As an Adult . . .
Who in your family do you compare yourself to?

_____

Who in your family do you contrast the most?

_____

Who enjoys *you?* _____

Describe a recurring memory involving your father, your mother, or both.

This memory bothers me because

How has this memory affected your life?

What strong feelings do you experience when you think of this memory?

What would your life be like if this remembered event had not taken place?

I **should/should not** put this memory aside, because
(circle one)

 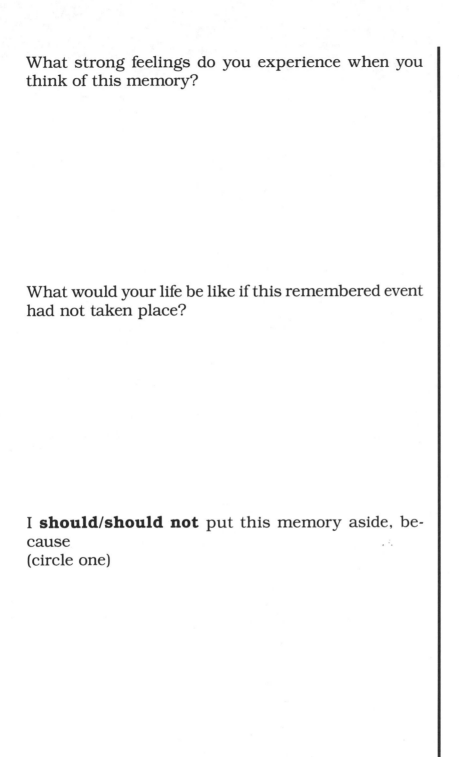

Would forgiveness change my story?

Now, run this parental memory through truth therapy.

• *Accept* the fact that your memories can be lying, at least a little bit.

• *Believe* the truth instead of the lies that are ingrained in your life-style.

• *Change* your behavior by using different self-talk.

Keeping in mind the positive influence of self-talk, repeat the following statements.

1. "I release you *(Mom, Dad, Mom and Dad)*. I am no longer a child. I am responsible for how I feel and respond to life."

2. "I release you *(Mom, Dad, Mom and Dad)* from the anger and hurt I have felt because of (name the problems) _____."

3. "I release you *(Mom, Dad, Mom and Dad)* from being responsible for my happiness."

If you find yourself having trouble with the idea of forgiving your parents, consider Jesus Christ, the Master Director of your life's play. Like the professional, detail-oriented stage directors of today, He knows the subtle difficulties of the role you are currently acting out. He knows the problems of your character far better than you, because He has occupied the very spot on Earth's stage where you now stand.

Nearly 2000 years ago, He lowered Himself, joined the cast of humanity, and became a part of this world's ongoing stage play of struggle and hardship. He did all of this and suffered much in the process so that He might better understand the complexities of *your* life. No one knows the conflicts of your onstage character better than Jesus: *"For we do not have a High Priest who cannot sympathize with our weaknesses, but was in all points tempted as we are, yet without sin"* (Heb. 4:15).

If you think that pardoning your parents will require more understanding than you possess, look to the Master Director as your model for strength. Christ's capacity for forgiveness is unsurpassed. Just consider the amount of indulgence the divine Son of God had to display in His choice of an adopted family tree.

The listed genealogy of Jesus recounted in Matthew 1:1–17 is an incredible roster of dysfunctional, fault-ridden characters. There is *Thamar,* who, posing as a prostitute, lured her father-in-law, *Judah,* into incest. The products of that union were the twins, *Pharez* and *Zarah.* Through Pharez, the sacred line proceeded. Then there was the Jericho inn keeper, *Rahab.* In the book of Joshua she is described simply as "a harlot." After her adventure protecting the two Israelite spies of Joshua's camp, she became the wife of *Salmon,* and bore him a son, *Boaz,* the great-grandfather of *David.*

If you think that pardoning your parents will require more understanding than you possess, look to the Master Director as your model for strength.

The adulterous affair King David had with *Bath-sheba* resulted in the murder of her husband, the crisis pregnancy and death of their firstborn, and eventually the birth of the great Israeli king, *Solomon.* In the line of Solomon was born *Joseph,* who took as his wife a young girl who he discovered was already pregnant. The result of the controversial, teenage pregnancy of that girl, *Mary,* was the supernatural birth of *Jesus Christ.*

Acknowledging the skeleton-packed closet of those parental memories, Jesus persevered. He is indeed well qualified to understand the problems which you have encountered with your parents. And if He, who was *"tempted like as we are, yet without sin,"* can choose to *forgive* and *live* with His human, mistake-filled heritage, surely you can find the strength to do the same.

It is time to heal those old, parental wounds and *pardon your parents.* Take the memory you described on page 176, and rewrite it, *after you have released those who have wronged you.* (Example: *Mom, Dad/ Mom and Dad, I realize that you hurt me when _____ but I am willing to forgive you because . . .*)

You must come to grips with the fact that things happen during childhood that should not occur. But it is up to you to determine how you'll deal with it. You can stay stuck in the past, pointing your finger at that person or event that wronged you and proclaim, *"There is the reason I am never going to do anything in life."* Or you can face that lie, examine your memories for the truth, and change your story.

If you can't pardon the mistakes of those who have played a role in your development, you cannot honestly forgive yourself. The only way to experience the process of healing is to run toward the hurt and face the truth.

You're no longer a child; you are an adult. Take responsibility for your life—how you feel and act. Like you, your parents are only human. Isn't it time you pardoned them? When you do, you'll find that you've let yourself off the hook too.

If you can't pardon the mistakes of those who have played a role in your development, you cannot honestly forgive yourself.

Once you've forgiven your parents for the mistakes of your childhood, the logical next step in your memory exploration is to examine your present character and discover how to improve your *adult* relationships. And in this age of skyrocketing divorce, the one relationship that *obviously* needs examination and care is that dual connection between man and woman, husband and wife.

Marriage is no different than any other of the staged scenes in your life. If you can unlock the secrets of your childhood memories, if you can adjust your personal perception, then you can change the course of *this* story too.

All you have to do is call your companion in to join you, turn the page to Chapter 7, and the transformation will begin.

Stage Direction #6: Patience

Patience is the only attribute in Peter's list of directions that your character *already* possesses in abundance. The difficult task here is not to attain patience, but rather to avoid losing it.

Why is it that whenever we are in the biggest hurry, everything seems to go wrong? Has this scenario ever happened to you?

For some reason this morning your alarm failed to go off, and you are late for work. So you sprint to the shower, hurriedly dress, and then make a dash for the family car. But as you are halfway out the door you discover that you have on two *different* shoes! Running frantically back into the house, you completely destroy your room in an effort to find the right pair.

Finally, you are in the car on the way to work, but now it seems that every traffic light in town is stuck on red. You start to perspire. Helplessly you check your watch and begin to wonder if the entire world is in a conspiracy against you. In an effort to gain control over these mounting circumstances, you impulsively stomp on the gas, swerve through an intersection, and abruptly lock fenders with a parked police car.

Sound familiar? Although this is somewhat of an exaggerated example, it clearly illustrates an important lesson: a *lack of patience can be extremely expensive!* Not only can it cost you time and money but it can rob you of your most valuable asset, your dignity.

When you lose your patience with a person or a situation, your character displays a blatant lack of control that is obvious to everyone. It causes the other players on your stage to look at you in a different light. And most of the time that new perspective is not positive. Whether or not the evaluation is justified is of little consequence if your personal worth has been compromised.

It always takes more energy to regain another's confidence than to lose your patience. It is too valuable a commodity to be tossed away over the silly inconveniences of everyday life.

If the attribute of temperance is ability to control your own actions, then patience is the elusive skill that governs how you react to the world around you. Once you have learned the art of maintaining your patience, not only will others perceive you differently, but you, too, will see the world in an entirely different light, as a team of amateur mountain climbers discovered.

The group was traversing the high elevations of the Swiss Alps when their guide happened upon a glacier grotto, a man-made cavern fashioned to shelter climbers from the frigid winds. It was a welcome sight, and the weary group quickly entered through a tunnel that burrowed through the solid ice.

"As we entered the chilly depths away from the outside sunshine," one of the climbers recalled, "the light became dimmer and dimmer. And when we finally reached the narrow chamber at the end of the passage, the darkness was as black as pitch."

"Wait," the climber recalled the guide whispering in the dark, "in five minutes you'll see the light clearly." The shivering men waited, and true to his word, in about five minutes, a light began gradually to appear.

"What happened," the climber explained, "was that our eyes gradually got accustomed to the new surroundings. The atmosphere brightened and soon the walls and roof of our ice cavern began to glimmer with a pure, translucent green glow. In the clear soft light that surrounded us I could easily recognize the faces of my companions and I was even able to study my guidebook. It's amazing, after we waited a while the whole place just lit up."

You may be fumbling in the dark for some missing piece of your life. . . . Stop worrying about it.

As these surprised climbers discovered, a little patience can reveal much. When you sit back and let "nature take its course," it is amazing what you eventually see. Utilizing the patience you already possess, you have the capacity of enlightening the perception others have of you. This promotes better communication and less reasons for impatience. When you deliberately take hold and make use of your power of composure, you always shine a little brighter in the eyes of others. The mountain guide's positive words are worth considering: "Wait, and you'll see the light."

When you haphazardly toss away your patience, you fumble around in the dark and run the risk of unnecessarily colliding with barriers. Inevitably, when patience succumbs to panic, someone always gets hurt.

In the course of your memory journeys, you may be fumbling in the dark for some missing piece of your life. The absent part may be a child, a parent, a husband, or wife. The timing of the situation may seem beyond your ability to control. If that is indeed the case, you need to *stop worrying about it.* This too shall pass. *The only thing anxiety can alter is your positive attitude.*

The circumstances may seem frustrating, but you must never get impatient. Allow your temperance (self-control) to restrain your powerful self-will and never take over and "direct" the scene yourself. You are the *actor*, not the *director*. Don't let the frustration of your surrounding situation steal away the valuable knowledge of your hope. Within you lies the uniquely personal virtue to actually create your own future, if you will only be patient.

The light of opportunity *will* shine, if you will simply wait. As the old saying goes, patience is indeed a virtue. It is a valuable attitude that helps you cope with things beyond your control, even that traffic light that never seems to change.

Chapter Seven

Adult Escorts and Cradle Robbers

*We can change Shakespeare's story
and give our love a matinee.*

Involving yourself in a relationship with another human being can be the most wonderful or the most frustrating experience of your life. A relationship is the coming together of two unique characters, two separate personalities who wish to share their time, their experiences, and their company with one another. When that balm of affection is given and received in mutual measure, nothing can compare to the bliss. Yet when that personal devotion is out of balance or suddenly removed, nothing can match the misery.

Kevin Leman suggests that in the beginning of a relationship, before you invite someone to dinner or before you accept someone's invitation, ask your potential companion to perform this simple task: *"Tell me about three of your earliest childhood memories.*" It is the quickest way to break the ice and the surest way to discover the basic nature of your dinner partner's character.

Now, if you think that such a ploy is a sly way to learn about a person, you're right. The word *sly* is just a euphemism for the word *wisdom*. And these days, when it comes to personal relationships, you need *all* the knowledge you can muster. Why? Because without exception, *we date the adult and marry the child.*

You can't deny that when you are out on a date, painting the town, you are on your best behavior. It's only natural. During those first few outings, we are all prone to hold in our tummies, pretend not to be hungry, and try to remember our Emily Post. In short, when we date, we consciously try to act like the adults we should be. However, that mature caricature quickly disappears once the props of marriage have been set out on the stage.

More often than not, just after the words *I do* are spoken, the phrase *never again* quickly enters your vocabulary. Remember, *the child you once were you still are.* As soon as you begin to feel comfortable in your marital bliss, that hibernating child inside you finally awakens, surprising your mate with a side of you never before seen. And the shock of discovering those "two children" so soon after the wedding often throws the romance off balance, right there at the start.

So we date the adult and marry the child. I guess you could say that we are all *adult escorts and cradle robbers.*

Whether you are dating, recently married, or baby-sitting your grandkids, it is never too early or late to find the balancing point between you and your companion. Relationships falter, not from a lack of emotion, but rather from a deficiency of communication. You can change the story of your relationship if you can learn to talk it out. Let's begin changing your story by reestablishing a link of communication between you and your partner.

For the following series of exercises, you will need two things: a pencil and your companion.

Take turns simply answering the following questions. Allow each other time to speak without being interrupted. Decide who will go first. Discuss how your views are similar or different. Most of all, enjoy this time together.

Relationships falter, not from a lack of emotion, but rather from a deficiency of communication.

- What was your favorite childhood memory?
- What do you fear?
- What unfulfilled accomplishment drives you?
- What does the word *peace* mean to you?
- Is there someone you have trouble loving?
- What hurts you most?
- If you had the power to change anything about the way you look, what would you change?
- What makes you happy?
- What is your favorite pastime activity?
- How important is communication to you?

Develop your own list of ten additional questions to build communication. Remember to respect one another's opinions and learn to see value in differing viewpoints.

List eight qualities you look for in a mate.

1. _____
2. _____
3. _____
4. _____
5. _____
6. _____
7. _____
8. _____

Out of these eight, how many does your companion have? List them.

1. _____
2. _____
3. _____
4. _____
5. _____
6. _____
7. _____
8. _____

Rate yourself: How many traits do you possess?

1. _____
2. _____
3. _____
4. _____
5. _____
6. _____
7. _____
8. _____

Name your partner's three most memorable childhood recollections. You do not have to give details, just a brief sketch. If you do not know his or her most memorable childhood memories, this would be a good project to do together.

1.

2.

3.

Since we date the adult and marry the child, fill in the following:

Male: Before Marriage

I acted like a child when I . . .   I acted like an adult when I . . .

Male: After Marriage

I acted like a child when I . . .   I acted like an adult when I . . .

Female: Before Marriage

I acted like a child when I . . .   I acted like an adult when I . . .

Female: After Marriage

I acted like an child when I . . . I acted like an adult when I . . .

You are learning things you never knew about each other. That's good. The more you know, the more you will grow . . . *Together*.

Twenty-Six Years: Still Strangers

Randy Carlson recounts a time at a memory exploration seminar when a woman approached him during a break and said,

"I've been married to the man sitting next to me for twenty-six years, and I don't know a thing about him. Would you ask him to share a memory?"

Glancing at the lady and her seated husband, Randy thought to himself, *"Great, you've been married to this guy all these years, you bring him to a seminar, and you want me to figure him out!"* Of course, Randy, being the pleaser that he is, told the woman he would try.

After the break, true to his word, Randy Carlson encouraged the husband to share a memory from his childhood. And to his inquiring wife's delight, he did:

"I was about three or four years old, I was in my bedroom. All I remember is the darkness of the room. I remember a priest coming in . . . a doctor coming in . . . and that I was sick. I remember feeling so alone and I huddled myself close to them . . ."

As the man finished, Carlson commented, *"That's exactly how you view life today, don't you?"* Tears came to the husband's eyes, and he looked up at Randy and sniffled, *"I felt so alone, that's exactly what my life's all about."*

His wife leaned over to him, put her arm around him, and said in a voice loud enough for all to hear, *"For twenty-six years I have lived with you and I never knew you felt that way."*

Each of you write down a memory that deals specifically with your relationships (platonic and/or romantic) during *childhood*. Read each other's memories out loud. Discuss them. Use questions from this workbook to guide you through those happy and sad recollections. Do not judge one another but allow for acceptance.

My childhood memory of love

My partner's childhood memory of love

Compare your stories, exchange questions.

List the emotions attached to this special childhood recollection. Be specific.

My Feelings   My Partner's Feelings

Memories of the Leman Tradition

When Kevin and Sande went to the Registrar's Office to get their marriage license, prankster Kevin couldn't resist having a little fun with his gullible bride-to-be. As they came up to the window, he said, "I just remembered an old Leman family tradition. The wife pays for the marriage license."

Sande looked at Kevin for a second and then responded, "Oh, how neat!" And she plunked down the five dollars. As they walked down the courthouse steps, Kevin grinned, "You've just started a wonderful tradition."

Each of you write down your version of your first date together.

Husband's version of first date with wife:

Wife's version of first date with husband:

Take the following quiz together. Place an X on the appropriate line indicating which character qualities you possess.

Responsible	__ You	__ Partner
Handles money well	__ You	__ Partner
Maintains a clear conscience	__ You	__ Partner
Patient	__ You	__ Partner
Loving	__ You	__ Partner
Tender	__ You	__ Partner
Listens well	__ You	__ Partner
Takes good care of self	__ You	__ Partner
Has a good relationship with parents	__ You	__ Partner

Forgiving	— You	— Partner
Sensitive to others' needs	— You	— Partner
Spiritual commitment	— You	— Partner
Enjoys children	— You	— Partner
Puts marriage first	— You	— Partner
Good sense of humor	— You	— Partner

Deleting the Walls

Marriage is supposed to be a joyous experience, a life of mutual discovering and sharing. But for many couples, all those hopes and dreams of the wedding day are now just hollow memories. Over the years, walls have steadily risen, blocking healthy communication. Instead of growing together, families are falling apart. And the barriers between husband and wife seem insurmountable.

One frustrated young wife who was starving for communication drug her husband, Gary, in to Kevin for counseling. Gary couldn't understand what was bothering his wife, he thought that everything was fine.

Relating one of his finest childhood memories, Gary told Kevin of being a boy of eight going fishing with his dog. He recalled opening his lunch bag and seeing his favorite treat, a peanut butter and jelly sandwich, with a big orange. No Zingers or Twinkies for dessert though. He recalled that his mom was always after him to eat healthy. Taking a bite of his sandwich, he remembered the pleasant solitude all around him. In his thoughts, he is alone and all is right with the world. . . .

What does this Norman Rockwell scene have to do with an unhappy marriage twenty-five years later?

Little Gary grew up to be a computer whiz, living with a working wife and two children who spend their days with a sitter. Gary devoted his time to solving computer mysteries. And at night after dinner, while Mom was catching up on parenting their attention-starved kids, he would shut himself away in the den and experiment with his personal Apple 2000. Only sixteen feet from his wife and children, but he might as well be sixteen hundred miles away on a river bank fishing with his dog.

At thirty-three, Gary's actions are consistently in line with his memories at age eight. He was good at amusing himself as a boy and he has kept it up as a man. His consistent theme was, *"You need to be in charge, and the best way to be in charge is to do it alone."* That maxim served him well—that is, until he got married. Now it was causing him all kinds of grief.

Gently, but firmly, Dr. Kevin Leman explained to the computer jockey the facts of family life, "Gary, you're married, and you've got two children. Betty works full time. What gives you the right to check out at 6:45 in the evening and not be seen again?"

Fortunately, Gary got the message. His computer-oriented mind kicked in, and he immediately started helping more around the house. He began with the dishes, then moved up to helping with the kids, and slowly, he managed to tear down the walls between himself and his wife.

Eventually, the computer whiz broke all the confining codes, deleted all the barriers, and gained direct access to the necessary pathways. Gary rewrote the software of his home life and, in the process, learned how to interface with his family once again.

What are the walls that threaten to divide your relationship? Name the ingredients that make up *your* wall (i.e., *the mortar of indifference,* the barricade of anger).

The hurdle of _____

The barricade of _____

The bricks of _____

The mortar of _____

The sand of _____

The concrete of _____

The walls between you and your companion, whatever they are made up of, keep you from hearing and feeling one another's needs. Next to each of the ingredients listed in the preceding exercise, describe the emotions you feel when experiencing that particular wall.

Hurt precedes anger. Walls are built piece by piece, layer upon layer. The frustration this causes often leads to anger and finally to an exploding point. Starting at the bottom with number one, transfer your "wall ingredients" to the numbers below so that a wall is formed. To the side, list any hurt, anxiety, or fear(s) that you have as a result of these walls.

10.   •

 9.   •

 8.   •

 7.   •

 6.   •

 5.   •

 4.   •

3.   •

2. Failing to be   • troubled over los-
   cherished   ing romance

1. Lack of time for   • hurt—I'm taken
   each other   for granted

Your wall may not reach all the way to number ten. The shorter the wall, hopefully, the less time it will take to tear it down. How many of the ingredients from the wall are part of your childhood experiences? Perhaps we do not feel satisfied or fulfilled inside. Maybe we are more like our parents than we realize, and we are bringing into the new relationship the un-resolved issues of our childhood.

Go back and circle those wall ingredients that were a part of your childhood difficulties.

Example: 1. *failure to manage household repairs: I procrastinate just like Dad*

2. *failure to listen to her: I never felt my mom listened to me*

Truthfully summarize your feelings about marriage.

Male
Marriage is . . .

Female
Marriage is . . .

Male **Marriage is . . .**	**Female** **Marriage is . . .**

What have you learned about each other that you didn't know?

Husband's insights:

Summarize your wife in five key adjectives (i.e., loyal, tender, sensitive, fearful, cautious).

1.

2.

3.

4.

5.

Wife's Insights:

Summarize your husband in five key adjectives (i.e., loyal, tender, sensitive, fearful, cautious).

1.

2.

3.

4.

5.

You Can Rewrite Your Story

Since we agree that Shakespeare was right and that all the world is a stage, then it logically follows that your life is a continuing series of scenes that are daily improvised. And if your life is made up of scenes, then your recurring display of thought, action, and emotion can truthfully be called a story, a play, a passionate vignette; a plot in progress.

Furthermore, if all the men and women on this world-stage are actors, and we actually do have the power to *accept* the truth about ourselves, *believe* in our strengths, and *adjust* our weaknesses, *then each of us has the ability to shape the plot of our own story.* It doesn't matter whether the story is about understanding yourself, facing the hard facts of your past, forgiving your parents, or confronting the troubles of your personal relationship; you can change the story. You are an actor on the world stage: the play you are performing is your life; and you possess the power of creative control.

A good example of this fact is displayed in the following verses. They portray how one man drew a parallel between Shakespeare's Romeo and Juliet and his own seemingly "star-crossed" relationship. The writer understands the power of forgiveness as well as the ability within each of us to choose and change.

Read the following verses and prepare yourself to make some choices.

Verona

The play was set in the town of Verona.
There, Romeo held a young girl's hand,
They whispered words of love to each other,
But the stars of fate crossed out their plans.

On my stage, stood a girl called Verona.
Playing my part, I placed a ring on her hand.
The lines we whispered spoke of love forever—
But like Shakespeare's pair, the stars had other
*   plans.*

Life is a play, and we're the actors, Verona,
So we can change what we say
And take it from the top again.
Life is a play—ours can have a long run,
*   Verona;*
We can give Romeo and Juliet a second chance
At love and life
Today.

If you take Juliet's potion,
If you leave our stage,

The stars will get the notion
They can always have their way.
Don't let our curtain fall—
I'm tired of audition, those cattle calls.
We can change Shakespeare's story
And give our love a matinee.

Just like Romeo and Juliet, your relationship with your family or your companion may seem star-crossed, hopeless. Yet throughout this workbook you have seen how to facilitate a noticeable transformation in your story. The fact that you have picked up this workbook in the first place proves your willingness to try. Therefore, whatever is wrong with your story, let's use the secrets you've unlocked from your childhood memories and facilitate *change*.

"The Play's the Thing"

In Shakespeare's "Hamlet," the young prince devised a stage play that confronted his uncle's life fact-to-face. By reenacting the scene in question, using painstaking detail, personal perceptions were altered, thereby adjusting the facts to coincide with Hamlet's current view of himself, his family, and his world. Hamlet's little play fleshed out the truth.

Like Hamlet, you, too, are going to reenact a play. Choose a scene from your memories that even today may seem hopeless, "star-crossed," irreparable. Based on what you have learned about your personal perception, positive self-talk, the ABC's of truth therapy, confronting the lies in your memories, and adjusting the facts, describe the event in painstaking detail. Then rewrite the scene based on how you view yourself *today!*

Who are the players in this scene? *(Mom, Dad, your best friend, your spouse, your children, a stranger)*

When did this scene take place?

Where did this scene occur? *(Home, office, in a park, in your car)*

Through the lens of your personal perception, describe the scene in as much detail as possible:

- What pivotal words were spoken and by whom?
- What pivotal actions were taken and by whom?
- What was your motivation? What prompted you to respond?
- What emotions did you feel?
- Who were the givers and takers in this scene?
- What actions could you have taken to direct this scene a different way?
- What was the result of this scene?
- Who was affected?
- Based on what you have learned about your personal perception, what possible "lie" does this scene portray?

If you *accept* that your personal perception misread this scene, what do you *believe* actually took place? *(Don't change the facts, adjust your perception of the event.)*

Forgive and Remember

The peaks and valleys described in these emotions are feelings you have already visited through your relations with your parents and your partner. And based on the knowledge you have discovered along your memory journey, there is no need for you to travel that road—and fall into those traps—again. If Christ can forgive those who turned against Him, He can give you the strength to do the same: *"Bearing* with one another, and forgiving one another, if anyone has a complaint against another; even as Christ forgave you, so you also must do" (Col. 3:13).

Nevertheless, it is important to remember how, what, when, and where you came from. Because unless you know how far you've come, you cannot measure how far you have yet to go. And there is so much that lies before you.

Unless you know how far you've come, you cannot measure how far you have yet to go.

Just ahead awaits your family—your children. Around the corner, there are countless scenes to be acted out in which *you* play the parent. Soon you will have another opportunity to correct the mistakes that you have recalled from your childhood. And though you have chosen to forgive those imperfections, *never, never forget them!* For as we will discover in chapter 8—just ahead—those who do not learn from the past . . . are destined to trip those parent traps again.

Stage Direction #7: Godliness

The seventh attribute on Simon Peter's list of stage directions is godliness. In many circles this word is used in a religious context. However, in the framework of your self-exploration, godliness is your character's higher point of view, which influences the development of your reputation—your integrity, your long-term choices. No matter what role you choose to play on the world's stage, the essence of this trait will always shine through. It is the most recognizable, defining part of your personality. Its natural qualities cannot be concealed, no matter how hard you try.

For instance, if Hollywood were inclined to remake "The Wizard of Oz," no director in his right mind would cast Madonna as Dorothy. No one would believe her in the role. Despite the fine performance she would most certainly give, her natural personality would clash with the wide-eyed innocence of her on-stage character. Why?

A person's true character cannot be submerged. Like a bright red beach ball in a backyard pool, it will always bob to the surface and stick out like a sore thumb. Therefore, to make sure that your character exudes the proper qualities, you must constantly check your priorities and monitor both your reputation and your point of view.

To attain the higher attribute of godliness, a sense of personal value and integrity, it is vital that you know the true motivations behind the long-term choices of your life. What is your treasure? What is "success"? How do you define "making a difference"?

The purpose of your memory exploration is to discover who you really are. It is to unlock the secrets of why you act and react as you do. One major clue in that discovery is the answer to the simple question How valuable is your life to you?

Everyone who has ever set foot on Earth's stage has, in some fashion, defined the word *value*. In the world of Entertainment and Sports, true worth is labeled "The Big Time." When young actors and athletes first attain this lofty goal, they are usually hit with the works: instant cars, money, sex, and fame. These are virtually handed to them on a silver platter the moment they sign on the dotted line. And for a time, they all enjoy the attention. But eventually a few wake up from their hangovers, come to their senses, and realize that there has to be more to life.

Upon taking a step back from the edge, each of these enlightened souls attempt to take stock of themselves and evaluate what is the most valuable to them. Eventually, they whittle things down to two basic choices: making money or making a difference. Given the makeup of their character, the majority choose the right path and go on to live fulfilled, productive lives. But, there are some who put their whole heart and soul into traveling the short road to success.

The majority of these hot shots are so blinded by the glitter of instant fame that they can't see tomorrow. All they seem to exist for is the moment and the roar of the crowd. These "blinded" individuals don't seem to aspire to anything higher than a theater marquis.

A few years down the road, when their looks start to fade, their muscles begin to give way, and their contracts run out, their short road will also end. They will have given their whole heart—and their one and only life—to that which they valued most. And all they will have to show for it is a "treasure" of dusty trophies, overstuffed scrapbooks, and the fading memory of a cheering crowd. Their collection of trinkets will have defined for posterity their version of the words *life, value,* and *worth.*

How valuable is your life to you?

Take a moment and think: *What is important to me? Is it my career? My family? My health? My home and possessions? My charity work? My free time? Is it making my house a home? Making a gourmet meal? Or is it making a definitive difference in the world around me? In the end, what is most important to me?*

Did you examine these things from the "higher" panorama of godliness?

From that lofty perch, far above the petty contrivances of earth's stage, you can see none of the trivial props of the stage—just yourself. Viewing your life from that higher perspective, what do you see?

Somewhere down the road, you will get your fifteen minutes of fame. After yours is spent and the final curtain goes down on your performance, what will the critics say? What will be the most valuable, the most memorable, portion of your time in the spotlight?

Here are some hints: It's as obvious as the color red. It weaves and bobs in relationship to the turbulence of its surroundings. You can try to submerge it, but it always pops to the surface. And no matter how hard you try to conceal it, it sticks out like a sore thumb.

It is your reputation. That is what people will remember.

If the true nature of your character does *not* possess the valuable attribute of godliness, the integrity to try to make a difference, the nobleness of a well-spent life, then you must ask yourself this one final question: What will the critics talk about for those fifteen . . . long . . . minutes?

Chapter Eight

Trip the Parent Traps

*"Those who cannot remember the past
are condemned to repeat it."*
—George Santayana

There is an old gospel hymn that asks the question, *"Will the circle be unbroken?"* The circle referred to here is obviously the family circle, that perpetual cycle of grandparent, parent, and child. In the great scheme of things, it is indeed important to perpetuate the family, to keep the heritage going. However, in order to keep the multiple layers of that cycle alive and productive, there is a particular ring in *your* family circle that you *must sever*—now! That is the vicious circle of parental mistakes passed down from one generation to the next.

That cruel circle must be broken to allow your family cycle to continue positively.

As the cycle goes, your parents were affected by the mistakes of your grandparents, and you were influenced by the updated version of those same traps. It is up to *you* to break that cycle, because the scenes you are acting out today are the memories your children will recall tomorrow. When they look back on their childhood, they won't see your parents—they'll see you.

Using the secrets of your childhood memories, you can uncover the parent traps that have been passed down and laid out for you like so many land mines. You can trip those traps and render them powerless.

An old Chinese proverb says, "If you don't change directions, you are likely to end up where you are going." The implication is clear: It is up to you. Only *you* can do the changing.

If you don't change directions, you are likely to end up where you are going.

Take heart! It is possible to avoid the mistakes of yesterday, change your family's ongoing story, and even transform the future memories of your children. All you have to do is break the family circle of parental mistakes, by tripping the traps your memories have set for you.

Vicki broke the circle, but it took time. When this expecting mother was asked to relate one of her childhood memories, she literally recoiled in a protective reflex response. The memories of this twenty-seven year old were so painful that it took her several minutes of silent struggle before she was able to speak.

I always had trouble in school, I never could keep up with the other kids. I recall being asked to come up to the chalkboard in the third grade to do a math problem. It was multiplication, I think. Well, I made a mistake, and the whole class laughed. I could have died. I was so embarrassed.

My first day of school was awful. I was so embarrassed when my stepfather took me into class. He was so drunk that he could hardly walk, and it was only 8:30 in the morning.

When I turned six, my mother gave me a birthday party. We were playing "Pin the Tail on the Donkey," I think. Well, my stepfather did it again. He didn't think I was doing it right, so he called me a whole bunch of names—Stupid, Dummy, and vulgar things I really don't want to repeat. He was always putting me down. I hated him.

Vicki's childhood left deep scars on her life. Every facet of her existence was affected by those early years. As she grew, she fell prey to the traps that await a person trying to run from a past of pain and personal abuse. Because she had no help from her family or any other support system, it was not surprising that she followed a series of trails that led down dead-end streets of divorce, drugs, and, on two occasions, almost death.

But then she met her husband, Jim, got into counseling, and underwent an emotional and spiritual renewal that helped her make real progress toward putting her life back together.

During her counseling, she learned from Randy Carlson how to change the personal perception of her memories with truth therapy. She also made slow progress with forgiving her drunken stepfather, who had made her childhood a living hell. The Law of Creative Consistency dogged Vicki like a hound on the scent. With her victim/pleaser life-style, she believed that she had to make everybody happy and never say no. Her life theme told her, "You're no good . . . You don't deserve a wonderful husband or your friends."

Randy helped her see that the lie in her life theme was being whispered by the little girl she once was, who was still living inside. "But now your rational, adult self knows better," Randy told her. "You have to take responsibility for your adult self and keep telling yourself the truth to counter those lies."

"You have to take responsibility for your adult self and keep telling yourself the truth to counter those lies."—Randy Carlson

As part of Vicki's therapy, Randy made it a point to talk to her about her expected baby and the parent traps that could easily interrupt her journey back to health. When they explored her early childhood memories, several recurring patterns became obvious, and any of them could threaten to show up in her own parenting unless she remained vigilant.

Vicki's list is one that all parents should consider. Study the following information, and file it away inside the storehouse of your brain under the heading

Tips on Traps

The trap of being too harsh. Vicki hated her stepfather and did not have a good opinion of her uninvolved mother. Nevertheless, her parents' example taught her how to be a parent. Under stress with her own kids, it would be easy for her to fall back into the same unhealthy pattern she had known from childhood.

The trap of discouragement. Vicki struggled with the self-talk notion that told her she couldn't do anything right. And by extension, she feared that she would become a bad parent. Once her baby arrives she is bound to have bad days, like everyone else. During those times, she could easily blame herself for the things that go wrong. Discouragement could set in, which, if left uncorrected, could lead to resignation and defeat.

The trap of demanding too much—or too little. Because Vicki's early childhood memories lacked balance, they were full of extremes and overreaction. When parenting her own children, she could easily go either way.

The trap of all talk and no action. Yelling and put-downs were the main form of discipline around Vicki's childhood home. In her present-day home the opposite approach is vital: healthy interaction along with a few well-chosen words of love and encouragement.

You may have experienced the frustrating paradox of vowing: "I'll never be like my mother (or my father)" and then find yourself repeating the same behavior you want to avoid.

To avoid these traps, take the following steps.

Identify the potential parenting traps in your own memories. If you can recall any of your early memories of how your parents disciplined you or didn't discipline you, record them in the space provided.

My memory of how I was disciplined:

The clearest part of this memory is

The feelings I attached to the clearest part of this memory are

The parenting style I might pick up from this memory is

Identify the potential parenting traps in your life-style. The following are some suggestions of the kinds of parenting traps different personality styles could face.

Pleaser

- Not challenging or confronting your children when necessary
- Being too permissive
- Being too easy to manipulate because you want your children to like you

Pleasers are not always passive. You may be the kind of pleaser who is more concerned about what friends and neighbors think than anything else. This could lead to

- Being too strict
- Setting perfectionistic standards
- Discouraginag your children with excessive demands

Controller

- Being manipulative
- Being a loving dictator
- Being a less-than-loving dictator
- Being authoritarian and even cruel
- Not taking time to explain your actions or to give reasons why
- Ignoring your children's feelings while concentrating on your desires

Charmer

- Wanting to be a kid yourself
- Not playing proper leadership roles
- Being inconsistent—seeming permissive one minute, authoritarian the next

Victim/Martyr

- Casting an aura of pessimism over the family
- Teaching your family the glass-is-half-empty view of life
- Wanting excessive sympathy from your family
- Feeling resentment because you feel that your children are taking advantage of you

Use the following four-letter codes in distinguishing which parenting type best matches the following statements. Be careful and attentive. Authoritarian—AUTH; Permissive—PERM; Hurried—HURR; Materialistic—MATR; Competitive—COMP; Neglectful—NEGL; Perfectionistic—PERF.

_____ 1. Overprotective parents tend to smother their children.

_____ 2. We'll do it our way.

   _____ 3. Our way is best.

   _____ 4. Children who grow up in this atmosphere feel helpless.

   _____ 5. Feeling inadequate is a result of this character trait.

   _____ 6. One parent is authoritarian and one parent is permissive.

   _____ 7. "You cannot do anything right."

   _____ 8. Not confronting your children about how to change.

   _____ 9. Not taking time with each child is a fault of these parents.

   _____ 10. Getting caught up in the rat race of life.

   _____ 11. Putting projects ahead of family.

   _____ 12. Having to keep up with the neighbors.

   _____ 13. Failing to meet the emotional and physical needs of each other.

   _____ 14. Forgetting to keep promises to your children.

   _____ 15. Demanding too much of each other.

(ANSWERS: 1–6, AUTH; 7, PERF; 8, PERM; 9, HURR; 10, COMP; 11, MATR; 12–13, NEGL; 14, HURR; 15, PERF. NOTE: More than one answer may be correct.)

Study your answers to the previous questions. What insights about your current home do they reveal?

Windows, the Dinner Table, and Mirrors

Kevin suggests that you can gain a good view of where you are as a parent, as well as where your children stand, by sitting around the dinner table. There, while you're dishing out the mashed potatoes, ask your kids in passing, "Hey, by the way, what is the earliest thing you can remember?"

Don't expect them to recall the trip the entire family once made to Disney World or the expensive gift you gave them on their last birthday. What will come to mind will be an event seemingly insignificant to you, but listen close! Their memories are a window into their world. Their recollections are also an excellent mirror for you to examine the kind of parenting *they* need *you* to display.

One of the best indicators of your parental performance is the reaction of your audience—your children. Read the following question and its possible answers to each of your children, and place a check mark next to the characteristics *they* agree with.

I often feel that my mother/father is . . .

_____ Too strict

_____ A perfectionist

_____ Too permissive

_____ Pessimistic

_____ Acting like a kid

_____ A follower, not a leader

_____ Permissive one minute and authoritarian the next

One of the best indicators of your parental performance is the reaction of your audience—your children.

_____ A dictator

_____ A "loving" dictator

_____ Ignoring my feelings

_____ Emotionally unapproachable

_____ A martyr

What specific memories of your parents' parenting skills still haunt you? Identify your parents' weaknesses. Place a check by the flaws you remember.

_____ Authoritarian—"The parents are always right and strict."

_____ Permissive—"The parents are not always strict."

_____ Hurried—"The parents are always on the go."

_____ Materialistic—"The parents buy more to solve problems."

_____ Competitive—"The parents compete for success and attention."

_____ Neglectful—"The parents do not act responsibly."

_____ Perfectionistic—"The parents expect perfection."

_____ Martyrlike—"The parents expect the children to take care of the parents' needs."

Now compare your previous answers with the potential weaknesses in your _present_ household. Check the flaws of your own parenting.

_____ Authoritarian—Always right and strict.

_____ Permissive—Not strict enough.

_____ Hurried—Always on the go.

_____ Materialistic—Money settles every dispute.

_____ Competitive—Winning is everything.

_____ Neglectful—"Kid's have to learn to do it themselves."

_____ Perfectionistic—"A-minus! You're grounded!"

_____ Martyrlike—"You'll be the death of me yet."

Based on the exercises in this chapter, what parental traps have you uncovered?

How do you intend to break the family circle of parental mistakes?

The Play Is Still the Thing

Once more like Prince Hamlet, you are going to reenact a play. This time choose a scene from your childhood memories, one that even today may seem hopeless, star-crossed, irreparable. Maybe it is a recollection of an event you hope that you, as a parent, don't repeat.

Based on what you have learned about your personal perception, positive self-talk, the ABC's of truth therapy, confronting the lies in your memories, and adjusting the facts, describe the event in painstaking detail. Then rewrite the scene based on how you view yourself *today!*

- Who are the players in this scene? *(Mom, Dad, your best friend, your spouse, your children, a stranger)*
- When did this scene take place?
- Where did this event occur? *(Home, office, in a park, in your car)*
- Through the lens of your personal perception, describe the scene in as much detail as possible.
- What pivotal words were spoken and by whom?
- What pivotal actions were taken and by whom?
- What was your motivation? What prompted you to respond?
- What emotions did you feel?
- Who were the givers and takers in this scene?
- What actions could you have taken to direct this scene a different way?
- What was the result of this scene?
- Who was affected?
- Based on what you have learned about your personal perception, what possible "lie" does this scene portray?
- If you *accept* that your personal perception misread this scene, what do you *believe* actually took place? *(Don't change the facts, adjust your perception of the event.)*

In the great scheme of things, it is indeed important to perpetuate the family circle, to keep that heritage going. Yet, in order to keep that cycle alive and productive, you *must* sever the vicious circle of parental mistakes that have been passed down to you from the previous generation. Because the scenes you are acting out today are the memories your children will recall tomorrow.

You must sever the vicious circle of parental mistakes that have been passed down to you from the previous generation.

Apply what you have learned and trip those traps. You *can* avoid the mistakes of yesterday and not only change the course of your story but give your children a collection of memories they will cherish . . . throughout the stages of *their* lives.

Stage Direction #8: Brotherly Kindness

"What is he doing here? Get rid of him! I will not be associated with such a gawky ape as that!"

Pretending not to hear the loud, harsh words, young Abraham Lincoln sat his lawyer's bag on the courtroom table and nonchalantly glanced at his pocket watch. He knew the insult was deliberately directed at him, but in spite of his mortification, Lincoln bravely thrust himself into the small cluster of attorneys, who, like himself, had been retained for the day's big court case.

As the trial got underway, Lincoln was virtually ignored. He did not sit with the other lawyers. Instead, off by himself, he listened as the attorney who had so cruelly insulted him, brilliantly defended his client. By Abe's evaluation his logic was masterful. The man's handling of the case held Lincoln spellbound. As he watched, the brash attorney cleverly manipulated the facts and before the day was done, he went on to win both the case and Abe's admiration.

His argument was a revelation, Lincoln thought to himself. *I never heard anything so finished and so well prepared. I can't hold a candle to him. I'm going home and will study law all over again.*

Time passed, Abraham Lincoln became the president of the United States. And among his most outspoken critics was the lawyer who had once spoken out so cruelly and cleverly. Nevertheless, in that time of civil war, when Lincoln again sat alone, the attorney's brilliance and brashness came to mind. Writing down the man's name, Lincoln placed it in nomination for the most pivotal cabinet position of the day, the one post which employed the necessary alliance of both reason and ruthlessness. Putting aside his personal feelings for the sake of the greater good, the president chose Edwin M. Stanton as Secretary of War. The two men worked side by side throughout the majority of the war, each depending more and more on the other's gifts. Stanton, a portly, bearded, bear of a man, came to admire the fellow he once called "ape," and over time, he found himself to be a better man for knowing him. In fact, this brash attorney who once proclaimed, "I will not be associated with such," went out of his way to meet with his superior upon receiving word of Lee's surrender. Announcing the news with an uncommon display of emotion, Stanton threw his large arms around Lincoln and expressed his admiration with an affectionate bear hug.

A week later, Lincoln and Stanton were separated once more. Although they were both in the same room, they were irreversibly divided—not by malice but by mortality. Lincoln had fallen victim to an assassin's bullet. It was now Stanton's turn to sit alone. And struck by the notion, "I can't hold a candle to him," the brash old attorney raised his voice with one last remark directed at Lincoln: "Now he belongs to the ages."

The historic changes in Edwin Stanton's attitude took place because Abraham Lincoln chose to exhibit brotherly kindness, an unmerited, but genuine regard for others. This particular stage direction influences one's character to consider the needs of others first, to apply the golden rule to every situation: *Treat others in the same way you wish to be treated.*

Lincoln had good reason to ignore Stanton. The president had every "legal" right to snub the attorney with the same unfeeling gusto Stanton had publicly expressed toward him. But the attribute of brotherly kindness within him opened his eyes to regard his adversary's redeeming qualities. And recognizing the great need of his country for such a man, Lincoln deliberately chose to overlook his own wounded character and do what was best for all concerned.

Choices create chances, not the other way around. Lincoln's decision to display kindness, unlocked a door of opportunity that would have otherwise remained shut. That open door opened eyes and promoted individual improvement and genuine affection between both men.

Had Stanton's negative opinions and Lincoln's hurt feelings not been resolved, it is quite likely that the larger conflict of America's two warring factions would have also, in time, become just as divided, separated, and disgruntled.

Brotherly kindness is the essence of unselfish consideration. It enhances your associations with the other actors on the stage. Its qualities produce the essentials for human harmony. Its traits promote the mutual caring and understanding of one another.

This necessary addition to your character is founded on a sincere mental attitude of concern and compassion. Indeed, brotherly kindness is acting toward others the way you would hope others would act toward you.

Recalling the past childhood scenes of conflict within your home, it is doubtful that any of the players ever voluntarily relinquished the stage to allow another to freely speak. Thinking back on those occasions, the attribute of brotherly kindness would certainly have

Choices create chances, . . . unlock a door of opportunity.

defused many of those incidents. And no doubt its traits would have been a helpful asset in curbing your own, personal conduct.

Take a moment and imagine yourself in the place of those with whom you have battled. Put yourself at the opposite end of that two-way street. Have you thought to consider the other person's point of view? To them, were you like Stanton—boisterous with your own opinion, not considering all of the facts?

Try to understand their reasoning. Be sensitive to the emotions they held dear. Brotherly kindness is treating your friends like family and your family like friends. A good illustration of this notion is found in the classic tale of a traveler from a distant place, called Samaria (see Luke 10:30–37).

As this good gentleman traveled the road from Jerusalem to Jericho, he came upon a man who had been stripped and beaten and robbed of all his money. What he did not know was earlier that day a priest, and then a Levite (a Jewish Temple assistant), had also passed by this same wounded gentleman. But instead of stopping to offer assistance, they had "crossed to the other side of the road."

Without giving a thought to his own schedule, the kind Samaritan had compassion on the victim and went out of his way to help. He poured oil and wine into the wounds and bound them. Then, he put the man on his donkey and took him to an inn, where he cared for him.

The next day, as the Samaritan departed the inn, he left money with the innkeeper for the expenses of the man who had been robbed. And he told the innkeeper that he would pay any additional costs the next time he passed by the inn.

The Samaritan did an extraordinary thing: he displayed the very ingredients that comprise the attributes of brotherly kindness. Like Lincoln, this helpful fellow put another's concern above his own, taking time to convey a deep, genuine concern for the injured man. His care and understanding went far beyond what anyone would expect.

The good Samaritan's humane act is a vivid portrayal of how each of us should administer our daily lives. The moral of this timeless tale is obvious: Brotherly kindness is not just a necessary attribute. Its acquisition in today's volatile world is a moral imperative!

When a family of adult individuals lives together under one roof, as so many do these days, there are bound to arise moments of disagreement. However, if the household is guided by brotherly kindness, each of the parties involved will instinctively consider the feelings of the others. Each individual will *think*, first, and be mindful of both their *deeds* and their *words*. A kind act and a soft answer have a way of cooling off heated situations. You need to stop and think *before* you speak. It's important that you consider *what* you say to others, and *when* you should say it. The soft, considerate qualities of this attitude turn away wrath. It makes mountains into molehills.

Therefore, do for others as you would have them do for you. Speak to others as you would have them speak to you. Consider the feelings of every actor on your stage, and you will soon see a big difference in the way the players treat you.

To gain possession of this noble quality, your deeds must display a persistent compassion for those who daily surround you. Consider the examples of Lincoln and the Samaritan. If you will exhibit a little *diligence* and *faith*, you can show kindness to your adversaries. Utilizing your knowledge, you can discover a positive use for your critics. Exercise your virtue, endeavor to go out of your way to help others. And when a situation shows signs of heating up, look at it from the higher perspective of godliness, engage your temperance and patience, and respond with brotherly kindness.

When you ultimately attain this unmerited, but genuine regard for others, your enemies may one day become your friends. But, whether they ultimately evolve into colleagues, or persist in their wounding assaults, if you will put aside your personal feelings and offer them brotherly kindness, there is only one comment they will hold as true in their heart: "I can't hold a candle to 'em."

Chapter Nine

Recollection Review

Now, take a look over your entire workbook. You have come a long way. Frankly, if you have answered every task as best you can, you have compiled quite a "diary." This workbook is the playbill for the past scenes of your life. You have the lead role and you are doing a fine job.

Your character development, stage presence, and overall presentation have come a long way. You have defined and redefined your character and gained a different perspective on the scenes you have played.

However, before the curtain closes on this act, we need to rewind your mind one last time and review the stages of your memory.

Start back at the beginning and look through all of the memories you have recorded. By now you should have some "composite pictures," much like a montage of still shots that speaks to who you are inside and out. Take a moment to evaluate what you have recorded. Then continue this review by describing your memories for the last time.

My early childhood memories said the following about me.

I am

Other people are

The world is

My present personal perception sees things this way.

I am

Other people are

The world is

Now dig into your emotions and talk about the changes you are currently making in your life.

Describe what your childhood memories have taught you about yourself and who you really can become.

I Used to Think of Myself as:
(List five negative adjectives.)

1.

2.

3.

4.

5.

I Now Think of Myself as:
(List ten positive adjectives.)

1.

2.

3.

4.

5.

6.

7.

8.

9.

10.

It is time to read the new reviews of this show! Fill in the blanks.

The audience was ecstatic over the obvious changes that have been made in the life performance of _____. The transformation could only be described as

When _____ was interviewed recently, many newly unlocked secrets were revealed. The star is quoted as saying, "This is what I did to change my performance. I simply

Remember your ABC's?

A = _____

B = _____

C = _____

Accept the fact that your memories can "lie" to you. Believe the truth about yourself, rather than your ingrained life-style. Change your behavior by using different self-talk.

Changing? Let's Talk About it

What is your self-talk G.O.A.L.?

I am (fill in your new self-talk)

"No matter what our _____ may tell you, no matter what your _____, you are _____ stuck with self-defeating behavior. The little kid you once were you still _____, but you can live happily ever after anyway."

"Out of my way, self-defeating behavior, I am not like you. I am changing. I am going to enjoy life. Get out of the way _____."
    (List any self-defeating behaviors on this line.)

Take time to compose a letter or a poem of thankfulness that expresses the joy and release you feel having "unlocked" your childhood memories. Write out your thoughts here.

Go back now and draw a circle around each word that describes you now . . . words you could not have used to describe yourself just a few weeks ago. Do you see? There *is* a change in your heart and mind, and it has led to new actions . . . to a new performance . . . to a new direction in your story.

Compose a letter to Dr. Kevin Leman and Randy Carlson. Let them know your thoughts about what is happening as you have "unlocked the secrets of your childhood memories."

Now, find a friend. Maybe that friend is your closest partner, your husband/wife, or someone dear to you. Share with them just one thing about what an "unlocked memory" can feel like when it faces truth. Don't expect them to understand all at once, because, like unlocking memories, understanding takes time.

Your life is far from a well-crafted script, it is, rather a series of well-intentioned yet often mishandled improvisations. The circumstances of the scenes you play are based on the combined experiences of every prior scene you have played. Yet, as you have learned in these pages, you have the decision-making power to adjust the thoughts, deeds, and emotions you portray.

God, the Master Director has cast you in a flexible, influential role. You have the power to control which way your scene goes, as well as the very words you say.

It doesn't matter if the scene is about understanding yourself, facing the hard facts of your past, forgiving your parents or confronting the troubles of your personal relationships; no matter what atmosphere the stage may display, with the Director's divine guidance, you can change the story.

Simply *accept* the truth about yourself and your surroundings. *Believe* in your character's multiple strengths, and *change* your ingrained weaknesses to avoid the consistent traps that have so often ensnared you and the inner circle of your family. Develop a G.O.A.L. to Get Out And Live, and continually work to improve your performance.

Give yourself a standing ovation! You have unlocked the secrets of your childhood memories. Now with the power of that knowledge, take control of the direction of your story. And allow peace to encompass not just your memories—but all the stages of your life.

Stage Direction #9: Charity

The final trait Simon Peter recognized in his list of character enhancements is the attribute of charity. This all-important step toward personal improvement demonstrates the power of love in its most unselfish form.

An individual can acquire all of the previously mentioned attributes of diligence, faith, virtue, knowledge, temperance, patience, godliness, and brotherly kindness; yet, if that person lacks charity, his quest for self-improvement is incomplete. This ninth and final attribute is by far the most potent. Charity, or love, is the catalyst that fuses all of the other endowments together into an indestructible, collective force. So important is this trait in its relationship to all of the others that the apostle Paul said, "Though I speak with the tongues of men and of angels, and have not charity, I am become as sounding brass, or a tinkling cymbal. And though I have the gift of prophecy, and understand all mysteries, and all knowledge; and though I have all faith, so that I could remove mountains, and have not charity, I am nothing. And though I *bestow all my goods to feed the poor, and though I give my body to be burned, and have not charity, it profiteth me nothing. Charity suffereth long [diligence, patience], and is kind [brotherly kindness]; charity envieth not [virtue]; charity vaunteth not itself [godliness, temperance], is not puffed up* (1 Cor. 13:1–4, KJV)."

This overwhelming force dispels such cliches as "Love is blind." In fact, when a person is endowed with the traits of charity, all the senses of their character are heightened—especially their insight, which becomes 20/20. Through the eyes of this special love, an individual is able to display a genuine compassion for others *despite* what they see.

Charity is the overwhelming desire to give of yourself without expecting something in return. However, these days, the world is somewhat of an ugly, selfish place. Too few of its inhabitants are willing to take the chance and exchange *something* for a possible *nothing*. No one, it seems, is willing to supply the demand unless they are sure of the return on their investment. The result of such selfishness is today's bankrupt society, devoid of love.

Everywhere you look there is evidence of this global lack of charity. In every corner of the world, there are nations playing the dangerous game of chicken. Recklessly, they are speeding toward one another with detest in their hearts and destruction in their clinched fists. Each hopes that the other will give in and demonstrate a little compassion. But no one is willing to exhibit charity first. No nation is prepared to display that kind of "weakness."

But which is truly weaker: the man who extends a caring hand, despite what others think, or, the man who holds in his true feelings out of fear for his reputation? (Even such a display of self-concern denotes an inward need for love.)

Everyone needs love! Sadly however, the most modern example of this truth is found in the empty lives of today's divided families. From the ghettos to the suburbs, people are all the same; each of us is searching for a way to fill up that void, that inner vacancy where charity belongs. Whether we openly admit it or not, each of us wants the other to be the *first* to give in and exhibit the love we all equally require. But something within our flawed, selfish characters keeps us motionless, silent, perpetuating the void.

For an actor there is nothing more excruciating than that kind of empty silence. Just imagine the discomfort of a performer having to face the torture of a silent, unemotional audience. As the spotlight illuminates his smile, he fully expects to hear the applause of the crowd, but there is nothing. In that instant of perceived rejection, the actor freezes. Although he's aware of lines needing to be spoken, his faculties suddenly shut down, leaving him in the unexpected grip of fear. Irrational though it may seem, in that moment, the loneliness within him is all too real.

The other actors on stage sense his frozen anxiety. Each one knows the familiar panic. At one time or another they have all experienced that silent, solitary void. Nevertheless, not one of them is willing to break character and offer his or her assistance. It seems that they, too, are equally afraid, overcome by the selfish notion that stepping out of character, will change the audience's perception of *them*.

The hush in the theatre is deafening. The frightened actor wants to move, wants to speak, but he can't. And the others won't. Eventually, because of such selfish actions, the play folds, the curtain falls, and the despondent performer, along with his "supporting" cast, is forced to vacate the stage.

This scene of selfishness and fear ended sadly (as real-life dramas of the same kind often do), but it didn't have to. All it would have taken to change this story's abrupt ending is for one of the actors to break out of his selfish character and willingly display a little charity: *"Love casteth out fear"* (see 1 John 4:18).

Like the stunned actor overcome by rejection, you may also perceive your life to be equally silent and immobile. The hushed atmosphere surrounding your home and family may appear devastating. And the sensations of disdain and loneliness you have inflicted upon yourself or others may indeed seem incredibly real. But don't wait for communication to begin with the others on your stage. If you do that, you may be waiting until your final curtain falls.

Now is the time to break the selfish nature of your character. It's time that you throw your fearful emotions to the wind and display the loving nature of charity. Doing so, your act of love will transform the silence on your stage. It will dispel the void of separation you feel inside you and around you. If you'll simply *decide* to make that initial effort, love will lead the way and even cast out your fear of trying.

Charity begins at home. Change begins with you and your willingness to love.

The catalyst of charity will empower you with the diligence to pursue a new direction for your life, and the proper knowledge to perceive which way to go. Love will help you attain the confidence, the virtue, to see yourself in a new light, and the brotherly kindness to shine that forgiving light on others.

Charity will provide you with the faith to believe that you can actually traverse the shaky plank of communication that separates you from your loved ones. And it will supply you with the patience and temperance to handle the dizzying height across that silent void.

Yet most of all, love will lead you to the godliness, the integrity, to recognize the true worth of your charac-

Whether we admit it or not, each of us wants the other to be the first to give in and exhibit the love we all equally require.

ter, and its ultimate, irreplaceable role on the world stage.

If you seriously consider the observations of the fisherman, Simon Peter, and apply these nine attributes to the daily performance of your onstage characters, you will be better able to see "afar off"—not only to the distant memories of your past, but to the bright future that awaits you.

If you will follow the stage directions Simon noted, you will indeed be better equipped to unlock the secrets of your childhood memories and change the course of your personal story. Peter knew what he was talking about. He observed these directions himself and applied them to the transformation of his life. And in doing so, he changed the very course of his still-recounted story.

If Simon Peter can elevate the role of a fisherman to such heights that his directions for life are *still* observed after two thousand years, just imagine the lofty elevations *your* performance can reach.

"For if ye do these things, ye shall never fall."

Dr. Kevin Leman

Author of fourteen books on family and marriage, Dr. Leman's best-sellers have sold millions of copies and include *The Birth Order Book, Making Children Mind Without Losing Yours, Sex Begins in the Kitchen,* and *Unlocking the Secrets of Your Childhood Memories* and *Parent Talk* (both coauthored with Randy Carlson).

A masterful communicator, Dr. Leman is an internationally known psychologist and humorist and is cohost of the nationally syndicated radio program "Parent Talk." He and his wife, Sande, have five children: Holly, 21; Krissy, 20; Kevin, 16; Hannah, 6; and Lauren, 18 months.

Randy Carlson

Randy is the founder and president of Today's Family Life, Inc., and Parent Talk, Inc.; the vice president of the Family Life Radio Network; and the cohost of "Parent Talk," a nationally syndicated radio program (the first national live, call-in program where parents talk to parents). He has written four books: *Unlocking the Secrets of Your Childhood Memories*—a best-seller coauthored with Dr. Kevin Leman—*Parent Talk* (also co-authored with Dr. Leman), *Father Memories* and the workbook *In My Father's Image.* A certified marriage and family therapist, he founded three full-service Counseling Centers, one in Michigan and two in Arizona. He and his wife, Donna, have three children: Evan, 14; Andrea, 11; and Derek (D. J.), 8.

Many thanks to Barton Green for his help in writing this book.